The Loving Arms of God

The Loving Arms of God

Written by
Anne Elizabeth Stickney

Illustrated by
Helen Cann

EERDMANS BOOKS FOR YOUNG READERS

Grand Rapids, Michigan ✢ *Cambridge, U.K.*

Text copyright 2001 by Anne Elizabeth Stickney
Illustrations copyright 2001 by Helen Cann
Published 2001 by Eerdmans Books for Young Readers
An imprint of Wm. B. Eerdmans Publishing Company
255 Jefferson S. E., Grand Rapids, Michigan 49503
P.O. Box 163, Cambridge CB3 9PU U. K.

Printed in Hong Kong
01 02 03 04 05 06 07   7 6 5 4 3 2 1
All scripture quotations are taken from the Holy Bible,
New International Version®. NIV®.
Copyright © 1973, 1978, 1984 by International Bible Society.
Used by permission of Zondervan Publishing House.

Library of Congress Cataloging-in-Publication Data
Stickney, Anne Elizabeth
The loving arms of God / Anne Elizabeth Stickney;
Illustrated by Helen Cann
p. cm.
Summary: A retelling of Bible stories illustrating God's relationship with his people
through the history of Israel, the ministry of Jesus, and the early church.
ISBN 0-8028-5171-1 (cloth: alk. paper)
1. Bible stories, English. [1. Bible stories.] I. Cann, Helen, 1969- ill. II. Title.
BS551.2 .S742 2000
220.9'505—dc21
00-23829

The illustrations were rendered in mixed media.
The text type was set in Aldine 401.
The display type was set in Calligraphic 421 BT.
The book was designed by Gayle Brown.

Contents

Author's Note

The Loving Arms of God is a book of Bible teachings. It is the story of God's relationship with his people. In spite of his people's wandering feet and haughty hearts, God works to bring them into fellowship with him. *The Loving Arms of God* tells the story of that developing relationship throughout the history of Israel, during the ministry of Jesus while he was on earth, and finally through the development of the early church.

Older children will be able to read the book by themselves, while younger children will enjoy having someone read the stories to them and talk with them about the pictures. The discussion questions can be used in family devotions or in a church or school setting. Their intent is to nudge readers to think about their own relationship to the One who is reaching out to them with strong and tender arms.

Introduction

Before there was music or art, before birds migrated at the turn of the seasons, before people climbed tall mountains, there was God. There has never been a time when God wasn't. He works for our good every day of our lives and in all the places we go. His goodness and power will last through all the ages of time and eternity.

We know that God exists, but we have many questions. How did God make the world? Why can't we see God? Why does God sometimes seem so far away from us?

We won't know some of these things until we are with God in heaven. But other things we can learn now. In the Bible we can read about how God has always cared for his people. In church we can listen to ministers and teachers describe God. In the world we can see the amazing things God created — fish, birds, forests, oceans, and people. When we hear his words and see his works, we can begin to understand God. We learn that God is wise, orderly, mighty, and loving.

This book is about people to whom God showed himself. These people felt God's love and power and heard God's words. They experienced God's concern and protection. And meeting God made them into different people — people who obey him, trust him, love him and each other, and live with hope.

As we read these stories, we too are meeting God. And once we have met God and understood his love for us, we too can experience change in our lives. We can become more like God. We can pray with confidence. We can tell others about God. To everyone who comes to these stories, God offers himself and says, "Look! I am making all things brilliant and new."

God Creates the World

What do you see when you look out of your bedroom window at night? A big maple tree? A dogwood tree in the middle of your neighbor's garden? Apartment buildings? Flashing lights? Stars?

We all have our own windows. We all have our own way of looking at the world. Some people see the world as a collection of beautiful things that have come together by chance. Some people think that nature is the power that holds the universe together. And others see a world that is full of the wonder and goodness of a loving Creator.

Adam

Genesis 1-2

It was morning in Eden.

The sun glistened on the leaves of the young trees, for the early dew had not yet dried. Brightly-plumed birds were waking up and calling out their delight in a new day. The garden was spilling over with colorful flowers — purple, pink, scarlet, orange, and blue. Ripe fruit hung heavy on the trees. Chimpanzees swung from tree to tree and reached their long arms to pluck their breakfast from the high branches.

Behind the trees in the grassy meadow, deer, rabbits, and antelope leaped and jumped while lions watched with sleep-heavy eyes. Farther in the distance stood a range of high mountains, guardians of God's beautiful garden.

Adam was happy. He knew many of the animals that lived in Eden with him, and he was not afraid of them. He had everything he needed. He could never run out of food with all the fruits and vegetables he had discovered. He knew the sun and moon, and he recognized many of the star patterns that filled the sky at night.

And he knew God.

He knew that God had designed and made that wonderful garden with all its creatures and vegetation, and he knew that God was loving and big and powerful and very, very good. Adam knew that he could call on God at any time and God would hear and answer him. There had never been a time when Adam had not known the loving presence of God.

Yet the world had not always been so beautiful. At one time there were no trees, animals, rivers, or oceans. There were no planets, stars, suns, or galaxies.

Then God began the work of creation. Like an artist who paints a picture, God began with an idea of what he wanted to draw. Out of his tremendous goodness and power he gave shape to those ideas. He created the heavens and the earth.

At first the world was empty, and the silence was deeper than anything anyone has ever experienced. Then God separated the land and the waters. He set the sun and moon in their places. He began turning the world around and around, making days and nights for us and seasons and years.

Still, the earth was rugged and sharp-edged. So God smoothed some of the rough mountains into rolling hills and covered them with grasses and flowers. He planted towering pines and spreading oaks, spiky palm trees and sharp-smelling cedars. He grew forests. He put dune grass next to oceans and lakes. He placed seaweed and coral and bulrushes in the waters.

It was now a beautiful world, and God called it "good." Yet there were more things to set in place. God put fish, eels, squid, dolphins, and whales in the oceans and tadpoles, salmon, and trout in the cold northern rivers. He made elephants to lumber slowly along, gazelles to leap, and eagles to soar among the clouds.

The world was now full of movement and sound. Rivers cascaded over cliffs in magnificent roaring waterfalls. Buffalo thundered in herds across huge flat prairies. At night the calls of coyotes filled the darkness when all the other animals were sleeping. Now and then a shooting star fell from the heavens, making a quick dash across the expanse until it was lost from sight.

And when God saw everything he had made he said, "It is good."

Only one part of creation was missing — people. God lovingly formed the first person, Adam, from the dust of the ground, breathed life into his body, and gave him a soul. Adam was someone made in God's image. He was not exactly like God, but he had some of the same interests and longings and abilities.

God told Adam to take care of the garden that he had placed him in. He told him to watch over the animals and get to know them. Adam obeyed God gladly and enjoyed the home God had given to him.

It wasn't long, however, before God understood that Adam was lonely. Adam could play with the animals, hold them, and care for them, but he could not talk with them or tell them his ideas and feelings. At night when he watched the great canopy of stars above him, the quietness was also very great.

So God created a companion and helper for Adam. He put Adam into a deep sleep, and like a skilled doctor God took one of Adam's ribs from his body. From that rib he created a woman, Eve.

When God looked down on Adam and Eve he knew that his creation was complete. He was pleased with the people he had made, and he called them his children.

Meeting God

Remember the Promises
"In the beginning God created the heavens and the earth." *Genesis 1:1*

Grow in God's Love
Think of a time when you have seen the stars at night. If tonight is a clear night, go outside and look at the sky. What do you think of when you see such a beautiful universe? What does it tell us about God?

Pray
Think of some fascinating animals and kinds of trees or plants. Thank God for each of them as you praise him for the wonderful world he made.

God's People Praise

In Eden, Adam and Eve must have been full of wonder at the incredible things God had created. Beauty and grandeur surrounded them everywhere. Delicate spider webs, heavy clusters of fruit, and piercingly bright stars all pointed to a mighty, wise, and loving Creator.

We don't know exactly what Adam and Eve were thinking in those happy days. But another person who trusted God and walked closely with him wrote down some of his thoughts about the glorious world God made.

Psalms

Psalm 65

David was a shepherd with keen eyesight. He spent weeks by himself tending his sheep on the hills of Judea. He knew how clouds looked before a spring shower and how they appeared later in the season when a heavy storm was coming.

David could pick out one of his sheep from among all the others. Each one seemed to have different eyes or a different way of holding its ears. And David knew the land. At night when he closed his eyes he still held in his heart the memories of the rivers, the rocks, the grassy places, and the shade trees he had seen during the day.

David knew that the beautiful sky and land and all the amazing creatures that lived in them were created by God. Everything that he saw reminded him of his loving heavenly father. "The heavens are like loud voices telling about God's glory," David wrote, "and the skies, too, speak of the great things he has done."

When David saw so much splendor around him, he wanted to say "thank you" for it all. He wrote many poems and songs similar to this one to describe his feelings of praise and thankfulness and to express his wonder at God's goodness.

Lord, you formed the mountains with power and strength.

You calmed the pounding waves with your mighty word.

And now, even the warring nations hear and obey your voice.

The world echoes with joyful songs wherever the morning dawns and the evening ends.

You are constantly caring for the land and overseeing its harvest.

You created streams that carry water to fields everywhere,

so that our tables overflow with bounty.

The year's harvest is ample only because of your blessing.

The carts and baskets of farmers are full to the brim because of you.

Even the desert produces in abundance.

The hills are glorious.

The meadows are full of sheep.

The valleys overflow with grain.

They are all praising you with gladness and joy.

Meeting God

Remember the Promises

"Let everything that has breath praise the Lord. Praise the Lord." *Psalm 150:6*

Grow in God's Love

How do you express your thankfulness to God in your home and at church? What are some ways you remember that God is the one who has provided us with so many things?

Pray

Thank God for providing you and your family with enough to eat and a warm place to sleep. Praise God for his power and greatness.

God's Wonderful Creation is Spoiled

"It was only a little lie."

"It was only a joke. I didn't know she would think I was serious!"

"Everyone else was doing it."

Have you ever heard comments like this? Have you ever made this kind of excuse yourself? We spend a lot of time explaining our actions. We make up many reasons why we did bad things, and we think that we can make them appear good.

But the truth is that sin is sin. Even a small act of meanness can ruin a friendship. Even a tiny step of disobedience can turn us away from God.

Eve

Genesis 3

Eve and Adam were happy together. They were busy exploring their garden home and learning about all the many plants and insects and animals they found there. They visited caves and seashores and meadows, and they tasted tangerines and pears and figs and hazelnuts. There was nothing they could not do.

Except one thing.

God told Eve and Adam not to eat fruit from a certain tree, a tree that he called "the tree of the knowledge of good and evil." The many other trees were so full of fruit that Adam and Eve had no reason at all to touch this one tree. And they didn't for a long time.

Then Satan entered the garden, disguised as a serpent. He wanted to see if he could make God's children listen to him. He wanted Adam and Eve to obey him instead of God.

Satan found Eve alone one day. He asked her a simple question: "Can you eat the fruit of any tree in the garden?" Eve answered truthfully that she could have any fruit she wanted, except the fruit that came from that one special tree. If she tasted it, she told Satan, she would die.

Then Satan lied to Eve. He told her that she would not die but would instead become more like God. She would begin to know all sorts of important things.

Eve thought about Satan's words, and they sounded good to her. She became curious about the tree. She wanted to know why it was set apart and why it was powerful. So Eve took a piece of the fruit from the tree called "the knowledge of good and evil" and tasted it. Then she found Adam and gave him some of it to try. "God has kept the best fruit from us," she tempted him. "And eating it will not cause us to die. You can see that I'm still alive."

Later that day God came to the garden looking for Adam and Eve. But they were hiding from him. They were ashamed because they had disobeyed their Creator. They had broken the rules of the one who loved them. Satan had been right — eating that fruit made them aware of things they had not known before. Since God had breathed life into them they had always known what goodness was. But now they also knew what evil was, for it had come into their hearts.

God was angry and sorry when he found that Adam and Eve had disobeyed him. He told them that they would have to leave that special place called Eden. They would begin to experience pain, and they would have to work very hard to grow their food. And one day they would die.

But God did not send Eve and Adam from Eden without hope. He used animal skins to make clothes for them to wear. This was a way of showing them that he would continue to provide for their needs. He warned Satan that there would come a time when one of Eve's descendants would crush his head. And even though Adam and Eve had lost their special closeness with God, he went with them as they left Eden. He never left them all alone.

Meeting God

Remember the Promises

"All have sinned and fall short of the glory of God." *Romans 3:23*

Grow in God's Love

What do you think the world would be like if there was no sin in it? What would cities be like? Would there be money? Police officers? Churches? Schools?

How do you feel when something you have made is broken or lost? How do you think God might have felt when his world was spoiled?

Pray

Even though we no longer live in a perfect world, God has promised never to leave us or turn his back on us. Thank God for being with you today.

God's People Work

How do you feel when your teacher gives you a long list of spelling words to study? Or when a parent wants you to clean your bedroom?

No one likes to work all the time, and sometimes people have to work very hard to produce even a little of what they need. This is a result of the "Fall" — the disobedience of Adam and Eve that brought sin into the world.

On the other hand, have you ever been so involved doing a craft or working at a skill in sports that you forgot what time it was?

Working hard and doing something well can be very satisfying. The effort we put into studying, practicing, and learning make possible all the things that we do and have in life. Our work is another of the fine gifts God has given to us.

Cain and Abel

Genesis 4:1-16

Adam and Eve had two sons. The firstborn, Cain, worked the land. He planted seeds and watered them. He weeded the long rows so that his crops were not crowded and could receive the sunlight they needed. Cain enjoyed watching the grains and vegetables grow and gathering abundant harvests each autumn.

Eve's second son, Abel, was more interested in livestock. He preferred to roam the hills with his loyal followers — his sheep and goats. He knew which ewes produced the finest lambs and which of the rams were ornery or mean. Year by year Abel saw the quality of his flocks improve, and that gave him great pleasure.

After some time had passed, Cain presented an offering to the Lord. He brought to an altar some of his wheat and corn and gave the bundles to God by burning them.

Abel, too, wanted to make an offering to God. He loved God so much that he wanted his gift to be the best it possibly could be. One spring he took the fattest of his young lambs to an altar and said to God, "You have given me so much that it is only right that I return some of my flocks to you. Thank you for all of my flocks, dear Lord."

God watched while the brothers made their sacrifices. He saw Cain's wagonload of grain and Abel's sheep and goats. But God also saw into the hearts of Cain and Abel. He saw that Abel's love for him was very great, and he accepted his sacrifice. He saw that Cain kept the best part of his harvest for himself. He said to him, "I can't accept the words you speak and the token gift you give to me unless your heart is also mine. Do what is right and I will see it. Give me the best fruit of your labors and I will be greatly pleased."

But Cain wasn't really listening to God's words. He didn't learn from Abel's example that all he had — even what he had worked during many long and tiring months to produce — really belonged to God. Cain wasn't interested in tilling God's fields. He wanted them to be his own.

It was a very dark time for Cain. In his anger and jealousy he plotted to kill his brother. One day he said to Abel, "Come out to the fields and see how tall my wheat is." Then, as soon as they were alone, Cain attacked Abel, beating him again and again until he was dead.

Soon the Lord came to Cain and asked what had happened to his brother. "How should I know?" Cain replied bitterly. "I'm not responsible for Abel, am I?"

God was angry with Cain. "You cannot hide your sin from me!" he thundered. "Because of what you did to your brother you must wander the earth. The ground will no longer be a fertile provider for you. Your years of plenty are ended."

So Cain roamed the world, looking for a place to settle down. His work was painful, and he became weary. People he met scorned him. But the worst part of his punishment was that never again did he have a close relationship with the Lord.

Meeting God

Remember the Promises

"Whatever you do, work at it with all your heart, as working for the Lord, not for men."
Colossians 3:23

Grow in God's Love

One of Cain's descendants, Lamech, had three sons. The first was a shepherd, the second a songwriter, and the third a toolmaker. These occupations represent three kinds of work that endure to this day: agriculture, the arts, and industry. Which of these kinds of work interests you? What kind of career do you think you might enjoy?

Pray

Ask God to be near you throughout this day and night, in all your work and play.

God Sustains the Earth

After a bridge is built, the engineer who designed it goes on to other projects. Maybe the engineer will visit it now and then, but the bridge will work without the help of the one who planned and constructed it.

After a gardener designs and plants a garden, his or her work is not done. Every week the gardener must take care of weeds that pop up. The garden must be watered and fertilized or it will die.

Parents of babies know that their job is only beginning. They spend long years caring for their children. Even when their children grow up and leave home, many parents write letters and make phone calls to let their children know that they are loved.

Do you think God is like an engineer who built the world then left it alone? Is he like a gardener? Or is he most like a parent?

Noah

Genesis 6-9:17

After Adam and Eve left Eden, they found that all the things that God had warned them about were true. They had to work hard to raise their crops, and they and their children sometimes experienced great pain. Outside of Eden people grew old and died.

For a long time Adam's children and grandchildren and their children and grandchildren tried to live in a way that showed God that they loved him. Then little by little, people started to do all sorts of bad things. People ate too much food, they drank too much wine, they stole from other people, and they forgot about God.

All of these things caused God to become terribly angry, so angry that he even regretted that he had made the earth and the people who lived on it. God is holy, and totally good. He cannot look at sin. Because the world had become a home for evil, God decided that he would destroy it.

Then he saw Noah.

Noah was the kind of person God had intended from the beginning. He loved God and tried to please him in everything he did. God was happy when he heard Noah praying and saw that the most important thing in Noah's life was his love for God. God did not want Noah to be destroyed, so he thought of a way to save him.

God told Noah that there was going to be a great flood, that water would cover the whole world. All the forests and grassy plains and even the deserts would be under water. No one would be able to live through the flood, God said. Not a single bird or animal or human could find a way to survive.

But then God told Noah that he would show him a way to escape.

Noah was to build an enormous boat, an ark, big enough to carry Noah, his wife, their three sons, and their three sons' wives. It would have to be big enough to hold the food those eight people would need for many weeks. And it would have to be big enough to carry animals — two of every kind of creature Noah could find on the earth.

What a huge boat that must have been! It took Noah and his sons a long time to find the trees and cut the lumber and then to build the boat, but finally it was ready. God told Noah that it was time to gather the food and animals into the ark, because the flood was about to begin.

Such a horrible thing had never before happened on God's beautiful earth. Noah was afraid when he saw the steel grey storm clouds gather and heard the first sheets of rain pelt the roof of the ark. But he was learning that God would not destroy someone who believed in him and served him. Noah was safe in the loving arms of God, safe in the wonderful ark God had planned for his protection.

It rained for a very long time.

The boat that once had seemed so big to Noah now seemed very small. It rained for a week, then two weeks, then three and four weeks. Noah and his family became tired of being in such a cramped space. They were tired of hearing the rain on the roof, and they were tired of all the noises and smells the animals made.

Then after forty days and nights of constant rain, the skies were silent. The endless torrents of rain and fearful groaning of the wind stopped. When Noah and his wife peered out of the ark they could see nothing but water. Their home and the homes of their neighbors and relatives were gone — all destroyed because of God's dreadful anger. They couldn't see a single piece of land to walk on. Not even a mountain peak was visible. Noah knew that he and his family could not yet leave the ark.

One day Noah took one of the ravens he had brought on board the ark to the side of the boat and released it. Imagine how happy the bird was to use its wings and once more be able to soar above the earth! But there was no dry ground for the raven to land on so it returned to the ark.

Later, Noah thought there seemed to be much less water around. He wondered if plants might be starting to grow somewhere in the distance, too far away for his eyes to see. So he took a dove this time and released it. Far away the bird flew, and when it came back it carried an olive branch in its beak. Noah and his family rejoiced, for the branch was like a message telling them that once again the earth would produce plants, grasses, and trees. There would be new food soon for the eight people and for all the animals.

When Noah released the dove the next week, it flew and flew and flew. Noah waited for a long time, but the dove never came back. Noah knew then that it was time to open the doors of the ark so the animals could leave, for they could now survive on their own. And very soon, Noah and his family would build new homes and plant new gardens.

God placed a rainbow in the sky to remind people of a special promise he was making. Never again would he destroy all the living things on the earth. He told Noah that he could count on the regular change of the seasons, and the orderly passage of days and months. Until the end of time, God said, he would watch over and bless the world.

Meeting God

Remember the Promises

"As long as the earth endures, seedtime and harvest, cold and heat, summer and winter, day and night will never cease." *Genesis 8:22*

Grow in God's Promises

Have you ever been stuck inside your house for a few days because of a snowstorm or heavy rain? What was it like? What did you do to pass the time? How do you think Noah and his family felt to be cooped up in the ark for such a long time?

What does a garden need to grow? What does a gardener have to do? What gifts does God send to help a farmer's crops or a gardener's flowers grow?

Pray

Thank God for taking care of the world and taking care of you. As you pray, picture in your mind God's strong arms cradling the earth and everything on it.

God's People Take Care of the Earth

If you hear news reports that pollution is soon going to destroy our rivers and lakes, killing fish and causing disease in humans, you will take care of the earth out of fear.

If you are an artist who appreciates the daffodils that grow in spring or the daisies of summer, you will care for the earth in the name of beauty.

And if you believe that God is watching over the world he created, making it a safe and nurturing place for his people to enjoy, you will care for the earth because you love God.

Noah

Genesis 8:20 - 9:17, Psalm 104

When Noah and his family finally left the ark after their long months of waiting inside, Noah thanked God for bringing them safely through the flood. It was only because God was watching out for them that they had not been killed along with all the other people on the earth. It was only because of God's plan and care for them that they had been saved.

Noah built an altar and burned on it sacrifices of thanksgiving to God. Then he watched as God put his beautiful rainbow of promise in the sky.

Noah looked at the world that almost sparkled under the rainbow. It was as if everything had been newly made. Each sapling and bud he saw was a fresh creation of a loving God. Each honeybee that buzzed was a reminder of the way God had protected his creatures and cared for his children. Each drop of dew was a picture for Noah of how God's judgment was softened by mercy. Noah felt like Adam in a new Eden.

And God, too, thought about Adam and Eve. He remembered the instructions that he had given to them on the sixth day of creation. He told Noah the same things he had told his first human beings.

"My will for you is that you have many children and grandchildren, so that the earth is filled with wonderful people like you. You will have authority over everything you see — the fish and the animals, the hills and the rivers. Take good care of all the gifts I have given to you. Use them well."

Then in obedience to God's commandments, Noah planted a vineyard. He measured straight and even rows upon the ground and planted tiny seedlings. He crafted arbors for the grapevines to climb. He watered and pruned them and waited. Noah had learned to be patient.

In time, his work produced an abundant harvest, and with joy and thanksgiving Noah and his family gathered heavy clusters of sweet-tasting fruit. They talked together about the marvelous way God had taken care of them and was continuing to watch over them.

God's people never forgot these truths. Each generation told the story of the flood to its children and remembered how God promised never again to send a disastrous flood to the earth. Hundreds of years after Noah died, one of his descendants in Israel would remember how God had cared for Noah's family and write this psalm of gratitude to God:

When you called out to the waters, God, they obeyed you.
When your voice thundered from heaven, they flowed where you directed.
The waters left the high mountains
and descended to the valleys where you wanted them.
You set a line that they cannot cross;
water will never cover the earth again.
Now, water has become a beautiful thing,
not something we need to fear.
You make the clear springs on the tops of mountains

and watch as they flow down to the riverbeds.

Now, gentle rivers quench the thirst of wild animals that roam the forests,

and also field animals tamed by farmers.

There is plenty of water

even for the birds of the air.

When they come to drink from a brook or stream,

they build nests in the branches of trees that grow by its side.

And the songs they sing are beautiful.

You look down from heaven and see that the earth needs nourishment.

You send gentle rain that brings forth fruit.

Grass grows for the cattle.

Plants grow for people to eat.

You send rain for food, for strength,

for gladness, and for joy.

Meeting God

Remember the Promises

"God blessed them and said to them, 'Be fruitful and increase in number; fill the earth and subdue it. Rule over the fish of the sea and birds of the air and over every living creature that moves on the ground.'" *Genesis 1:28*

Grow in God's Love

What do you and your family do to take care of the earth? What sorts of things could you begin doing to be even better caretakers of the earth and its creatures?

Pray

Ask God to help you learn how to care for your home, your neighborhood, and your world. Ask God to give you a keen mind at school as you learn about God's creation.

God Calls
His People to Change

When a classroom gets a new teacher in the middle of the school year, everyone has to make changes. The new teacher may change former routines and schedules, and the class has to learn how to get along with someone with a different personality. When a new leader is elected to a government, that leader often makes changes too. Perhaps taxes will increase, roads may be fixed, and new schools and parks built.

When God becomes the leader of individual people, or families, or nations, God asks them to change how they see themselves and how they live.

Abraham and Sarah

Genesis 12, 15, 17, 18:1-15, 21:1-7

A man named Abram lived with his family in Haran. Sometimes Abram felt crowded at Haran. He was responsible for many people, and he worked hard making sure that their sheep and goats had enough water to drink and land to graze upon and that the land produced grain for his family's food.

One day God spoke to Abram and told him that he was going to provide a new home for him with more land than he could imagine. God promised that he would bless Abram abundantly. If Abram would choose to trust God's leading, his family would become wealthy and happy.

This was wonderful news to Abram! He wouldn't have to worry about being crowded anymore. Immediately Abram built an altar to the Lord to show God that he would trust and follow him.

Soon Abram and his wife Sarai and all their servants were packed and ready to leave Haran. They were eager to get to the wonderful new home God had promised to give them.

But it was not an easy journey. They traveled for many weeks to get to the place named Canaan that God had chosen for them. They ran out of water to drink and once had to go all the way to Egypt to find some. Sometimes Sarai wished that they were at home in Haran, doing all their familiar tasks, talking with old friends, living the life that they had been used to. Abram tried to encourage her. "We started this journey with God, and we'll keep following God wherever he takes us."

Then finally the drought ended, and the day came when Abram and his family arrived at Canaan. God told Abram and Sarai, "Look in all directions: north, south, east, and west. All of the land you can see — and even more — will be yours. Because of your faith in me I have chosen to bless you. I will make your family into a wonderful and special nation. And you, in turn, will be a blessing to the rest of the world because you will tell them about me."

Abram was deeply thankful for all the things God had given to him — a safe journey from Haran to Canaan, good health, and acres and acres of fertile land. Abram was quick to thank God for all of those wonderful blessings.

Yet one thing troubled him. God kept speaking of a new nation coming from Abram's family, but he and Sarai had no children. They were both getting older. Sarai was beyond the age when they could expect her to be able to bear children. How were God's promises going to come true?

God reassured Abram. He told him that he and Sarai would have a child, and their descendants would number more than all the grains of sand by the seashore.

Again Abram questioned God. How could this be true since he had no children and was already old? God told him that if he could count all the stars in the night sky, that number would not be as great as the number of people that would one day be born to Abram and Sarai's family. Abram still did not understand how this wonderful promise could be realized, but since he loved God he tried to believe his words.

Then one day, as Abram was sitting near the entrance of his tent, he saw three travelers coming near. Abram was eager to please them and be hospitable to them. He and Sarai rushed to make bread and prepare meat for the guests' meal. The visitors seemed very important, somehow different from anyone they had ever met. Before they left, one of the strangers said that Sarai would soon become a mother. Because motherhood would change her so deeply, she would have a new name, Sarah. And because Abram was to become a father, he too would have a new name, Abraham.

At first Sarah could not believe this news. She laughed at the visitors' words. But, incredibly, Sarah and Abraham indeed became parents that year. A healthy baby boy was born to them, and they named him Isaac. How happy the two parents were! They had trusted God, and God had changed them from a childless old couple who were common farmers into wealthy landowners with a blessed child. When they looked at Isaac's infant eyes, when they saw him walk by himself for the first time, when he said his first few words, they knew that God's promise to make a very big nation from their small family could really come true.

Meeting God

Remember the Promises
"Is anything too hard for the Lord?"
Genesis 18:14a

Grow in God's Love
What are some of the ways that God has blessed your own family?

Pray
Thank God for the many ways he makes your life better. Praise him for his blessings to you and your family.

God's People Answer

We know that after many centuries Abraham's family became enormous. Trying to count all the people who are descended from Abraham would be like trying to count all the grains of sand you see on the beach or to count all the stars in the sky on a clear evening.

Abraham and Sarah's family includes us, too. Everyone who believes that Jesus is God's Son has been adopted into that special family. We have become a part of God's dearly loved people. God calls us just like he called Abraham, and we, too, have the privilege of answering him.

Abraham and Isaac

Genesis 22:1-18

God saw that the birth of Isaac had made Abraham happy. After so many years of waiting, he enjoyed being a father very much. He loved to hear Isaac's laughter when he raced with other children. Abraham loved to tell the stories of the trip from Haran to Canaan and how God had blessed their family. Already he was imagining the many strong grandchildren that Isaac would give him.

God was happy for Abraham, but he wanted to make sure that Isaac had not taken over the special place in Abraham's heart that belonged to God alone. He wanted to make sure that Abraham was still listening to his voice.

One day God called out to Abraham and gave him difficult instructions. "Take your son, your only son, Isaac, whom you love," he said. "Go to the region of Moriah, and sacrifice him to me. Show me that you love me more than you love anything or anyone else."

And Abraham answered God. He didn't ask, "Why do you expect such a hard thing of me?" He didn't whine, "If you loved me, God, you wouldn't ask me to do this." He didn't even try to present God with a logical argument, like, "How are you going to make me the father of many nations if you take away my only son?"

Instead, Abraham answered God by calling Isaac to his side and packing for the journey to Moriah. His actions said, "I love you, God. I trust you and will do what you ask of me."

It was a hard journey. Abraham had a lump in his throat the whole time. Whenever he looked at Isaac's face he had to turn away quickly. Abraham kept his eyes on the sky as much as he could, trying to understand the Lord whose voice sometimes came from there. But he had to watch his footsteps on the rocky path, and his gaze was most often downward.

Finally Isaac turned to his father and asked, "We have everything we need to make a sacrifice to the Lord — the wood to burn, and the coals to light the fire. Yet I don't see the sacrifice itself. Where is the lamb we are going to offer to God?"

Fighting back his tears, Abraham answered, "God himself will provide the lamb for the sacrifice, Isaac. He will provide."

Then, when the trip was completed, Abraham made all the preparations. He took Isaac in his arms and held a sharp knife high in the air, ready to do what God had asked of him. Then he heard the voice that he loved most dearly of all voices he had ever heard. "Abraham," God said, "You have shown that your love for me is greater even than the love you have for your only son, Isaac. Do not harm him. See, over there in the bushes is a ram caught by its horns. Take it and sacrifice it to me in Isaac's place."

Tears streamed down Abraham's face as he clutched Isaac to him. "I spoke the truth," he murmured. "God did provide the sacrifice."

Meeting God

Remember the Promises

"Here I am! I stand at the door and knock. If anyone hears my voice and opens the door, I will come in and eat with him, and he with me." *Revelation 3:20*

Grow in God's Love

Think about whether God's voice is the one you love most dearly of all. God is still calling his people to lives of obedience. What are some ways that we can answer his call? How can God's people say "yes" to God?

Pray

Thank God for calling you to be his child.

God Helps His People

Sometimes we need help to get things done. A librarian helps you find information for a report at school. A parent may help you with a school project. Perhaps a friend helps you with your chores. When other people work with you, the task gets done faster and usually better than if you worked alone.

God is our helper too. He gives us the ability and strength to work at our tasks. He sends other people to give us things that we need. When God helps us we can do things that would otherwise be impossible.

Joseph

Genesis 37, 39-41

Jacob, a grandson of Abraham and Sarah, had twelve sons. All twelve of them loved Jacob, but Jacob loved one of his sons, Joseph, more than the others. Joseph was very handsome and reminded Jacob of his beautiful wife, Rachel. One day Jacob ordered a coat to be made for Joseph. It had brilliant colors and looked splendid enough for the wardrobe of a prince. Jacob gave the coat to Joseph simply because he loved him. He probably didn't think how all the other brothers would feel when they saw the beautiful new coat.

Joseph's brothers were enraged.

They thought they all should have such a beautiful coat — or else none of them should. They were tired of seeing that Jacob favored Joseph. And sometimes they didn't like Joseph very much at all. Being spoiled had made him proud. He told the ten older brothers about dreams he had dreamed. "I am more important than you are,"

Joseph told his brothers. "My dream told me that someday you will all bow down to me." The ten brothers complained to Jacob, but Jacob still favored Joseph.

One day when they were far from home tending sheep, Joseph's older brothers saw Joseph approaching, dressed in his fancy coat. He was bringing them a message from their father.

"I can't stand living with Joseph any longer," said one of the brothers. "I wish he were dead," added another. And then, together, the ten of them decided to do something that none of them would have dared to do by himself. They decided to kill Joseph.

When Joseph came with Jacob's message, the ten brothers hit him and punched him, yelled at him, and spat at him in their anger. Joseph, outnumbered, was powerless against them. He would surely die.

But then Reuben, one of the brothers, became frightened at the power of their hatred and said, "I've had enough of this. Let's not kill him yet. Let's put him down the old pit that is over there. He'll be dead soon enough." Privately, Reuben thought that he would come back by himself later to free Joseph.

The others respected Reuben and listened to his plan. They ripped the special coat from Joseph's shoulders and threw him into the deep and dark pit. Then they killed a goat and dipped the coat in its blood, deciding that they would tell their father that Joseph had been attacked and killed by a wild animal.

Before the brothers turned towards home on that awful day, they saw a caravan nearby. The camels belonged to slave traders who were on their way to Egypt. When the brothers told the traders about their younger brother, the traders offered to buy Joseph for twenty pieces of gold. That was a great amount for those brothers who only rarely saw coins, so they were happy to pull the bruised and frightened Joseph out of the pit and sell him for a handful of money.

When they arrived home they told their father that Joseph had been attacked by a wild animal. They handed Jacob the stained coat, telling him that it was all that remained of Joseph. Jacob mourned deeply for his dearest son.

God watched over Joseph on the journey to Egypt. He saw him working hard in the household of one of Pharaoh's assistants. And then he saw him thrown into prison because of a disagreement with the wife of his employer. God never left Joseph alone through all those difficult years.

After Joseph had been in prison for a long time, Pharaoh was having strange dreams that troubled him greatly. He dreamed that seven fat cows came up out of a river to a field of corn and ate it all. Then seven lean and scrawny cows came to the field and ate all the plump cows. Pharaoh asked his advisors if they could tell him what it meant. No one at court could understand it at all. Then the butler, who overheard Pharaoh speaking of his dream, remembered that he had once had a dream which had been correctly interpreted by a man who was in prison with him.

"Go and find that man and bring him to me!" Pharaoh ordered his guards.

Joseph was still in prison, probably bored and frightened, but also trusting that the God of his father and grandfather was with him. When Joseph heard of the strange dream about the cows and corn, he was able to tell Pharaoh its meaning.

"There will be seven years of plenty in Egypt," he told Pharaoh. "All the fields of your country will produce a great bounty and no one will be hungry. At the end of those years, however, there will be seven years of hunger and need. Those are the seven lean cows in your dream."

Joseph spoke with certainty, and Pharaoh did not question his words. "What can be done to prevent the famine?" he asked.

Joseph answered that he could do nothing to stop the seven lean years from coming, but if they planned wisely, they could save enough grain during the years of plenty to see them through the hard times. Pharaoh appointed Joseph to be in charge of his storehouses and to see that enough food was put away to last through the seven years of drought.

Once again, God had rescued Joseph and given him a new beginning.

Meeting God

Remember the Promises

"Where does my help come from? My help comes from the Lord, the Maker of heaven and earth." *Psalm 121:1b-2*

Grow in God's Love

What are some times when we need God's help? In what ways do our government, churches, and social service agencies help people with special needs? What are some ways that individual people can help them too?

Pray

Thank God for the times he has helped your family, such as during an illness or a move to a new neighborhood. Thank him, too, for the people he has sent to help you.

God's People Help Others

Imagine you are driving at night during a huge snowstorm. The wind is blowing the snow so fiercely that it is almost impossible to see. The driver of your car swerves suddenly to avoid another car, and you end up in the ditch. After you wait twenty minutes or longer, another car sees your red taillights and stops to help you get back on the road.

After you thank the person who helped push you out of the ditch, you get back on the road. When you have driven along in the cold darkness for two or three miles, you see another car stopped with its nose pointed downwards into the ditch.

What would you do? Stop to help the stranded people, or keep on driving?

Joseph

Genesis 42-45

For seven years Egypt was a happy place. Rain fell often. The fields produced more grain than anyone had seen harvested before. Joseph made sure that part of the harvest each year was saved for the dry years that he knew lay ahead, and he carefully watched over the builders as they made new buildings in which to store all the grain.

The eighth year was a terrible year. The farmers planted their crops in the same way as they had in the seven years of good harvests, but there was not enough water to make things grow well. The harvest was very small. Had it not been for Joseph's careful planning, everyone in the country would have been hungry. Instead, they were able to get food from the supply that had been saved during the years of plenty.

Those countries that had not been warned to save some of their food quickly ran out. The leaders tried to stretch what they had to feed everyone, but for many weeks and months people in the countries surrounding Egypt, including Canaan where Joseph's family lived, were hungry.

Egypt's supply of grain did not remain a secret for long. Caravans traveled east across the desert bringing word to Jacob of an unimaginable amount of food that Pharaoh had stored up. Jacob's sons saw their children's big hungry eyes and knew that they must go to try to buy some of that food. Jacob did not want to let them go, but soon he realized that there was no other choice. Without help from Egypt's Pharaoh they would all starve.

When Joseph's ten older brothers arrived in Egypt, they were taken to see Pharaoh's overseer — Joseph himself. He was a man now, not the young boy they had beaten and betrayed. He was dressed in Egyptian clothes and spoke the Egyptian language. His brothers did not recognize him.

Joseph knew his brothers immediately, but he did not tell them who he was. He was glad to see them, glad that they were still alive, and eager to hear news of their father and youngest brother Benjamin. He gave them plenty of grain and sent them on their way back to Canaan. But he told them there would be no more grain unless they brought Benjamin with them next time.

When their food supply was again very low, the brothers returned to Egypt, this time with Benjamin. Joseph almost wept with happiness when he saw his younger brother — the one closest to him in age and his special favorite. But he still did not tell his family that he was Joseph. Instead, he used trickery to convict Benjamin of stealing. He had his servants hide an expensive goblet in Benjamin's pack. When he later uncovered the goblet during an official search, he told his family that they could return to Canaan but that he would have to imprison Benjamin.

The older brothers did not dare to return home to Jacob without Benjamin, who had become their father's favorite in Joseph's place. They pleaded with Joseph to spare Benjamin's life. If they didn't take Benjamin back to Canaan, they told Joseph, their father would die of sadness.

Something made it impossible for Joseph to keep his secret any longer. Perhaps it was thinking about his dear father grieving for Benjamin. Or perhaps it was seeing the change in his brothers. Once they had sold a young brother into slavery; now they were pleading for the life of another one. Joseph told all the Egyptians of the court to leave. He then told his astonished family that he was their brother, Joseph.

With a mixture of happiness and shame, the brothers embraced Joseph. They were happy that Joseph was safe and had become an important man in Egypt, yet they felt guilty for the way they had treated him years ago. Seeing their sorrow, Joseph reassured them, "Don't think any longer about how I came to be in Egypt. God wanted me to be here all along, so that through me he could help you during these years of famine."

Joseph told Pharaoh about his brothers, and Pharaoh gave them carts and donkeys laden with food to take back to Canaan. "Fill the carts with your families and all your belongings," Pharaoh told them. "When you return I will give you the best land in Egypt for your own. Because of your brother Joseph I welcome all of you into Egypt."

Meeting God

Remember the Promises
"I tell you the truth, whatever you did for one of the least of these brothers of mine, you did for me." *Matthew 25:40*

Grow in God's Love
How do you feel when you help one of your parents or a teacher? Have you ever helped a younger child learn or practice a skill? Did you enjoy that?

Pray
Think of people who are going through a difficult time. Pray for them, asking God to show you ways that you can help them.

God Leads His People

Have you ever been lost? Maybe you became separated from your mom or dad at a store. Or perhaps you went for a walk with a friend in overgrown woods and couldn't find your way out. Maybe during your first week of school you got lost in your school building.

In situations like these, we need someone to take us by the hand and show us the way. We need someone to lead us home.

Moses

Exodus

The family of Jacob stayed in Egypt for many years. They did not return to their homeland in Canaan even after the famine had ended because they were happy in the prosperous land that God had helped them to find.

After several generations, however, the people of Egypt no longer remembered Joseph or the pharaoh who had been so friendly to him. They did not remember that it was a person from Israel who had warned their country of the dreadful years of famine. The Egyptians looked at the nation of Israel and saw that they worshiped an unfamiliar God and practiced many different customs. They made fun of the Israelites and eventually made them their slaves.

These were hard years for the Israelites. They yearned to leave Egypt and return to the beautiful land that God had promised to Abraham and his descendants. In their despair the people of Israel cried out to God.

God heard their prayers and protected a special baby, Moses, so that he would be able to lead his people out of slavery. Moses was saved from Pharaoh's army by a princess, who then raised him in Pharaoh's court.

In many ways, Moses was an Egyptian. When Moses became a man, however, he could not ignore the cruel ways that the Egyptians treated the people of Israel. One day he saw an overseer beating a Jewish slave, and Moses was so full of anger that he killed the Egyptian. After that he never returned to his easy life in Pharaoh's court. Instead he became a shepherd in far-distant regions.

Yet after several years had passed God told Moses to return to Pharaoh and to ask for the freedom of the people of Israel. Moses knew Pharaoh well enough to know that he had good reason to be afraid of him. So he made excuses to God. "I am a slow speaker, Lord," he told him. "I cannot think of the right words to say when it is time to say them." God replied that he himself would be with Moses and would help him with every word.

Still Moses was afraid. "There are far better men in Egypt than I, Lord. Send one of them." God was displeased at Moses' unbelief, but he told him that he could take his brother, Aaron, with him to Pharaoh's court. Aaron would do the talking for Moses.

When Moses and Aaron came to him, Pharaoh could not be persuaded to release the people of Israel. Moses and Aaron told Pharaoh that unless he let the Israelites go God's anger would be released against him. Still Pharaoh refused.

God kept his word, and his anger was terrible. Grasshoppers, frogs, boils, even death — all sorts of catastrophes happened to the people of Egypt, and in desperation one night Pharaoh said to Moses, "Go! Leave Egypt and return to your homeland." Moses told the people of Israel, God's chosen people, to pack quickly and prepare for the journey.

The Israelites took many things with them to the land of Canaan — their jewelry, as much food as they could carry, tents, animals, and clothing. One thing they didn't have, however, was a good map. Their nation had been away from home for so long that now they had only a hazy idea of where it was they were heading.

But God did not abandon the people of Israel. He told Moses he would put a pillar of clouds into the sky. That pillar would show them the direction in which they should journey. At night, the clouds would be replaced by a pillar of fire. What a wonderful demonstration to his people that God was with them, guiding them every moment of their journey home!

In only a few days, however, Moses and the people of Israel were confused and discouraged. The pillar of clouds had led them to the shore of the Red Sea. In the distance behind them, they could see Pharaoh's powerful armies following them. Pharaoh had changed his mind about letting them leave Egypt.

"We're already running out of food," the Israelites complained to Moses. "If Pharaoh doesn't kill us now, we're all going to starve! Weren't there enough graves for us in Egypt? Why did you bring us out here into the desert to die?"

Moses was a very wise and powerful leader, but he knew that his power came from God alone. Moses turned to God and asked him what to do.

"Hold out your staff over the Red Sea," God told him, "and I will open up a path for you to take through it. Tonight I will protect you from Pharaoh's armies by sending my angel and putting the pillar of clouds in front of them. The soldiers will not be able to see or harm you."

And it happened just as God had said. When Moses held his staff over the sea a strong wind came up and formed a pathway through the water. God divided the water into two sections. Then he made a strong wind dry up the ground in the middle of the waters so that when the Israelites traveled on it, the wheels of their wagons would not become stuck.

When the clouds lifted, Pharaoh and his armies saw that the Israelites had safely crossed through the sea on dry ground. Quickly they urged their horses to follow them to the other side. But the special route was not meant for the Egyptians. When they were halfway across it, the water flooded the path and all the riders and horses and chariots were destroyed.

For a time the people of Israel stopped complaining, and they rejoiced at the way God had led them out of slavery into freedom. They recognized the miracles he had performed for them and praised him for his goodness.

Meeting God

Remember the Promises

"Jesus answered, 'I am the way and the truth and the life. No one comes to the Father except through me.'" *John 14:6*

Grow in God's Love

What would it be like to move to another country? How would it feel to leave familiar things behind you? Would you feel nervous? Excited? Happy? Sad?

Pray

Sometimes we only think about God when we are going through difficult times or when we have to make important decisions. But there is never a time when we don't need God to show us the way. Think about your plans for the rest of today and tomorrow. Pray that God will lead you in all that you do.

God's People Obey

If you were to get a new puppy, the puppy would have many things to learn: how to come when called, to sit when asked, and to stop chewing on your slippers or your project for school. You might take your puppy to obedience classes, where you could both learn how to get along.

We, too, have to learn that some of our actions are destructive, while others lead to health and happiness. We need to learn to obey our God who leads us.

The Ten Commandments

Exodus 20:1-17, 32-33:6

After the people of Israel had left the land of Pharaoh they had many questions to ask God. None of them had ever seen their home country. They had only heard about it in old stories passed down through the generations. They had lived among people who worshiped many gods, and there were pictures and statues everywhere of these gods that people could see and touch. Why was the God of Israel different? How should they worship this God that they could not see?

One day God called Moses to the top of a great mountain. The presence of God came upon the mountain like an enormous cloud. Then God told Moses, "I am going to give you ten laws for my people. Take two large rocks and write down these laws on them, so the people of Israel will read them and remember."

These are the commandments that the Lord gave to Moses:

Remember who I am — the God who saved you and redeemed you. I am the only
  God there is.

All the power in the universe comes from me. Don't make statues or pictures of
  things I have made and worship them and think that they have power to
  help or to heal you. Do not worship anyone or anything but me.

Speak my name with reverence and respect. Make sure that everything you say
  honors me.

Rest on the Sabbath day from your normal routine. Spend time worshiping me and
  thinking about what I have done for you.

Respect your parents. Obey them, be polite when you speak to them, and be careful
  what you say when you talk about them to other people.

Do not kill another person, or wish another person would die. I am the giver of life.
  Remember that life is precious.

Take care of the body I have given you. Do not hurt it or use it in a way that hurts
  other people.

I will take care of all your needs. Do not steal what does not belong to you.

Do not lie to other people or to me. Be careful what you say, because your words
  will tell other people what kind of person you are.

Don't spend your time thinking about your neighbor's possessions and wishing you
  could have them. Be thankful for what you have, and enjoy the life I have
  given you.

While Moses was meeting with God on top of the mountain, the people
of Israel grew impatient. "Why is he taking so long up there?" they murmured
to each other. "What's going on? Why can't we see this God? Every other nation
has a god they can touch and see."

After a few more days had passed, the Hebrews collected all the gold they
could find — earrings, rings, bracelets, and coins. Over a great fire, they melted

all the gold together and then crafted the figure of a calf from the liquid metal. "Finally!" they said, "we have a god we can see who will help us and hear us." And they bowed before the idol and worshiped it.

When Moses came down from the mountaintop he saw the golden calf, a useless idol just like one the pagans would make. Moses was angry. He was so angry that he smashed the precious stone tablets on which the law was written. "Is this how you thank the Lord God who brought you out of slavery?" he asked. "You deserve nothing more than what this hunk of metal can give to you."

Then Moses led the people in prayers of repentance. "We acknowledge that you are the one, true God," they prayed, "and that you alone are worthy of our praise."

God forgave his people for their idolatry and gave Israel another set of tablets with his law etched upon it. "Remember my instructions," God told them. "Think about them night and day, so that you learn to obey me with your words and thoughts and actions."

Meeting God

Remember the Promises
"Turn from evil and do good; seek peace and pursue it." *Psalm 34:14*

Grow in God's Love
What does the word "commandment" mean? Do we still have to obey these commandments, since Jesus has died to forgive us all our sin?

Pray
Ask God to take away the things from your heart that prevent you from obeying him — things like stubbornness, pride, and self-pity.

God Talks to His People

The nations that surrounded Israel — the Egyptians, the Philistines, the Canaanites — worshiped false gods. They made something they found in nature into an idol. Or they carved a statue and called that object holy. They prayed to these idols, and acted as if the idols were powerful and helpful. But the idols could not respond. They were useless objects that could not affect the lives of those who worshiped them.

How different those false gods are from the God of Israel who created us, cares for us, and speaks to us!

Samuel

1 Samuel 1-3

Hannah was a woman who felt like Sarah, Abraham's wife. She had everything she wanted in life except a baby. As year after year went by, she watched other women cradling their babies and carrying them to the well. She watched toddlers grow into girls and boys who played and teased and told stories. Still, Hannah's own arms were empty.

Yet one year, in answer to a special prayer from the priest, Eli, God sent a son to Hannah and her husband. Even before he was born, Hannah told God that this baby would be his in a very special way.

Hannah lovingly raised her son, Samuel, for two or three years, and then she took him to Eli, who served God in a quiet and holy place named Shiloh. Hannah was very thankful for the gift of Samuel, and she demonstrated that gratitude by giving him back to the Lord. For the rest of his life, Samuel would be a servant in the house of the Lord.

Yet even though Shiloh was holy and set apart from everyday life, it was still not a perfect place. Eli, the priest, had two sons, Hophni and Phinehas, who everyone expected would take over Eli's duties when he grew old. But Hophni and Phinehas were evil men. They did not trust God but lived only for themselves. When the people of Israel brought their sacrifices to Shiloh, Eli's sons demanded that they give them a large portion of the meat before it had even been presented to God. It was a tradition for the priest to take for himself a forkful of each sacrifice after the meat had been boiling awhile, but Phinehas and Hophni wanted more than a forkful of each sacrifice. They also demanded that it be roasted with all the flavorful juices sealed in, not boiled until it was tough and tasteless.

The Lord was angry with Eli's two sons, and Eli knew it. He tried reasoning with Phinehas and Hophni. He became angry with them. But nothing worked. They continued to cheat and lie, and they were not sorry for their sins. Eli was unhappy with them, but he permitted them to continue to help him at the temple. In the end, he loved his sons more than he loved God.

There was someone at Shiloh, however, who loved God more than any other person or any other thing — Samuel, the son of Hannah. He knew that he lived in a very holy place. He knew that all of his tasks at the temple were performed for God.

Samuel's bed was a small cot in a room next to Eli's. One night, Hophni and Phinehas were gone, and the temple was deserted except for himself and Eli. In the middle of his sleep, Samuel heard a voice calling to him.

Samuel knew that there was only one person who could have called him. Yet when he got to Eli's room to see what he wanted, he found that the old priest was soundly asleep. Samuel wakened him. "Why did you call me?" he asked.

"I didn't call you," Eli answered. "Go back to bed."

When Samuel had again settled himself for the night, he heard his name called again. "What is it, Eli?" asked Samuel when he approached Eli's side a second time. "Why did you call me?"

"You must be imagining things!" Eli told him. "Go back to bed and try to go to sleep."

Obediently Samuel returned to his room and tried to fall asleep. Eli also tried to sleep, but he was worried. Samuel was not the kind of boy to cause trouble. Perhaps there indeed had been a voice calling "Samuel." Eli knew that no one in the temple had awakened Samuel. There must be another explanation for the voice.

When Samuel came a third time to Eli's side, claiming that he had again been called, Eli was awake and waiting for him. "The voice that is calling is not mine," said Eli. "It's God's. If you hear him again, you must reply, 'Speak, Lord, your servant is listening.'"

How fearful Samuel and Eli must both have been in the darkness of the temple! Eli was the priest. If God had something to say, why wouldn't he tell it to him directly? Was God angry with him? And Samuel, though his heart was pure and full of love for the Lord, was overcome by the greatness of God. Could it be that God, the creator and ruler of the world, the Holy One of Israel, wanted to speak to him?

A fourth time Samuel heard his name spoken in the deep stillness of the night. Trembling, he managed to say the words Eli had told him to say: "Speak, Lord. Your servant is listening."

God's message to him that night was about the priesthood of Israel. God told Samuel that because of the wickedness of Hophni and Phinehas, and because of Eli's failure to control them, he would take the important job of being a priest away from Eli and his family forever. "Nothing can atone for their sins," God told Samuel.

It was a harsh message, but it was the word of the Lord. Samuel repeated every word the next day when Eli demanded to be told what Samuel had heard in the night. Samuel remained at Shiloh for many years and kept on living in a way that pleased God. God was very close to Samuel, and he spoke to him for as long as he lived.

And Samuel always recognized his voice.

Meeting God

Remember the Promises

"Speak, for your servant is listening." *1 Samuel 3:10b*

Grow in God's Love

We hear many different voices. Think of all the voices you have heard since you woke up this morning. (Don't forget the radio and television!) How can we hear God's voice today?

Pray

Thank God today for all the ways he talks to us.

God's People Listen

If you have ever gone to school and sat in a classroom for more than a few days, you have probably heard a teacher say, "What I say is going in one ear and out the other!" Maybe one of your parents uses that expression when at the end of a day you still haven't done a task you were asked to do that morning, even though you were reminded about it at least three times.

We can read the Bible every day and sense the voice of the Holy Spirit within us but still not be good listeners. God wants his words to change our lives. He wants us to hear his words and then make them our own.

Proverbs

Proverbs

Solomon lived a good life. He was born a prince, the son of Israel's beloved King David. He knew luxury and favor from the day of his birth. He was never hungry or unsure where he would find his next meal. When he became king he controlled more money than any single person in Israel had ever seen. It was his honor to oversee the building of the first permanent temple in Jerusalem — something God's people had longed for since the time when they were delivered from Egypt.

King Solomon's life was good not only because of all his silver and gold, but also because he had great wisdom. He knew that people must always remember that God created them and they live under God's authority. Solomon knew that doing whatever we want whenever we want leads not to happiness but to despair and death.

When he was older Solomon wrote down some of the things he had learned about how to live a good life:

Listen to your father, remember what he tells you to do, and don't forget your mother's years of teaching.

If you want to be foolish, ignore the advice of those who have traveled your road; turn away from the strong arm that reaches out to help you, and reject the one who is calling you by name.

Don't ever forget what God has asked of you, remember his commandments, for they will help you live longer and better.

This is important! Listen carefully!

Keep these words close to you, for they will be light in the darkness, and health for your entire being.

First of all, keep your heart pure, do not give it to anyone less than God or your life will wither and fade.

Stop talking critically and negatively.

Keep your eyes focused on your goal, and your way will be easier.

Keep your feet on the path you know is the right way.

Don't be distracted by what seems to be pleasing but is really masking evil.

Wise people surround you, listen to them! Follow their directions, remember what they tell you, and you will learn to trust in the Lord and follow him.

Meeting God

Remember the Promises
"My sheep listen to my voice; I know them, and they follow me." *John 10:27*

Grow in God's Love
Can you remember a time when someone gave you advice and you didn't follow it? What happened? Who are some wise people you can learn from?

Pray
Start today's prayer with Samuel's words, "Speak, Lord. Your servant is listening."

God Rules His People

Most people don't like it when others tell them what's good for them. We like to make our own decisions and get what we want. We sometimes think that no one else could know what is best for us.

But we often get in trouble when we live this way.

Saul

1 Samuel 10:17-24

Ever since God's people had left Egypt, God had been their leader and helper. He had given them food in the wilderness on their way to Canaan. He had protected them from their enemies. When Israel had a special need, God had given them a leader to help them in that crisis. Then for several years God had given Israel judges and priests to direct the people in the way he wanted them to live. And the nation of Israel had grown strong and wealthy.

Yet the Israelites saw that all the countries around them were ruled by kings, and the Israelites wanted to be like them. They liked the idea of grand processions and mighty chariots. They loved God, but they couldn't see him. If they had a king, they would see him, hear him, and even touch him. The king could lead them to great military victories, and the name "Israel" might become famous throughout the world.

Or so they thought.

When the people told Samuel about their desire for a king, Samuel didn't think it was a good idea. He was now an old man and wise from all his years of listening to God.

"We are not like all the other countries," Samuel told the people. "Our king is the Lord God himself."

"But we want a king who will lead us in battle against our enemies," the people replied. "A king who will bring glory and power to our country."

Samuel was frustrated with the stubborn people. "Can't you see how a king will change your lives?" he asked them. "He will demand a portion of all your goods. He will take your sons into his army or will demand that they build great palaces for his use. He will have your daughters work in his kitchens to prepare feasts for him. Nothing will ever be the same for you. Your whole lives will be centered upon the king."

"That's exactly what we want!" the Israelites insisted.

With a troubled heart Samuel took their request to God. "I tried to reason with them, Lord," Samuel prayed, "but still they say that they want a king."

"It is not you they are rejecting," the Lord answered Samuel. "Once again Israel is rejecting me. They do not want to live according to my plans for them. They want to rule themselves. Tell them that I will give them what they have asked for. I will appoint a king for Israel."

The Lord told Samuel to gather the people of Israel in one place, and from all the thousands of people he would choose the one who would be their king.

What an exciting day for Israel! When the sun set that night, they would know the name of their new king. As the families sat on the hillside, there was an air of celebration and festivity. Everyone was talking. They wondered what family the king would be from. They wondered if he would be someone old or young.

Samuel let the people talk among themselves for awhile. Then he stood before them and waited until there was total silence. In a loud voice he announced, "The new king will be from the tribe of Benjamin!"

All eyes turned towards the hillside where Benjamin's family was gathered. "A Benjaminite!" the people gasped. What excitement the members of that tribe felt!

Could it be a cousin, an uncle, a brother? Some, perhaps, even dared to wonder, "Could it be me?"

After the tension had mounted still further, Samuel announced, "Your king will come from the Matrite family!" There were cheers and applause, and when there was silence once more, Samuel told the people, "The Lord has chosen Saul, the son of Kish, to be your king."

"Saul! Saul! Saul!" the people chanted and cheered. "Show us King Saul!"

Benjamin's family looked for him on the hillside, but they could not see him. "Saul, where are you?" they called. But they heard no reply. "Where is Saul?" they asked each other. "When was the last time you saw him?"

Finally they found Saul far away, hiding behind the donkeys and packs they had brought from home. "Didn't you hear us calling you?" they demanded. "Why are you here with the baggage?"

Then Saul stood up, and all the questions of the people of Israel were silenced. Saul stood a head taller than the rest of them. He was strong and undeniably handsome. Here was a worthy king for their country.

Saul himself did not feel worthy. He knew that he was an ordinary man. He knew little about fighting wars and less about being the leader of armies. If he was to be Israel's king, he knew that he could not do it on his own. He would have to have God's daily help.

As priest, Samuel would still be an important person in Israel, but from now on the people would look first of all to King Saul for leadership. Samuel told Saul that he must continue to serve the Lord with all his heart. He must not worship false gods. He must continue to fear the Lord and pray to him for guidance. He must never forget that Israel's only true ruler was the Lord God.

Meeting God

Remember the Promises

"How awesome is the Lord Most High, the great King over all the earth!" *Psalm 47:2*

Grow in God's Love

Do you agree with the people of Israel who thought that having a king would be a great advancement for their country? What would you like or dislike about having a king? What characteristics make someone a good leader? Can you name a leader who has some of these characteristics?

Pray

A special Jewish prayer addresses God as "King of the Universe." Use that name for God as you begin your prayer today.

God's People Depend on Him

When astronauts orbit the earth on a small shuttle or space station, or when they shoot beyond earth's gravity to the moon and farther, they are not flying alone. They are constantly talking to flight directors and technicians on the ground. Even when the astronauts are sleeping, their computers are connected to computers on earth that track every mile of the space mission.

An athlete who wins gold medals at the Olympics depends on his or her coach. A surgeon depends on nurses who assist during operations. A school bus driver depends on mechanics who keep the bus running safely.

And all of us depend on the Lord.

David

1 Samuel 17

Two armies were encamped around the Valley of Elah. The Israelites, God's people, were on a hill on one side of the valley, and the Philistines were on the other. They were not fighting — yet.

For forty days one of the enemy soldiers taunted Israel. "Send one of your soldiers to fight me," he roared. "Whoever beats the other will win the victory for his entire army. Is there a man over there brave enough to wield a sword against me?"

For forty days the answer was "no." The Philistine soldier who appeared before them each morning with his proud challenge was over nine feet tall! The man who dared to fight him would be a fool, the Israelites thought, for no one could possibly overtake him in battle.

Or could someone?

One morning David, the youngest son of Jesse from Bethlehem, came to the valley with some grain and bread for his older brothers who were fighting in King Saul's army. David was talking with his brothers and some others when Goliath, the Philistine, paced along the line of his own army and roared his challenge at the Israelites.

"Someone must get rid of him!" David said. "No one should be able to defy us, the army of the living God!"

David's words spread quickly along the line of the Israelites until they reached King Saul. He demanded that the one who had spoken so courageously be brought to him. When David appeared in front of Saul, he told him, "I will fight that giant, King Saul. I will win the victory for the Lord's army."

Saul doubted that this could happen. How could such a young man defeat the seasoned warrior who towered over everyone on both sides of the valley? Saul was sure he would be sending David to his death.

David reassured Saul. "The Lord will deliver me. He saved me from the jaws of the bear and the jaws of the lion. Surely he will also save me from Goliath."

Saul gave David his own armor and helmet and sword to wear in the combat. But when David put it all on, he could barely walk. "I'm not used to this," he told Saul, "and it is too heavy." So David took off Saul's coat of armor. He went to the shore of the river and chose five small smooth pebbles for his slingshot. David knew that it was not the size of his weapons that would win him victory. He knew that God alone would protect and defend him.

When Goliath saw David coming near he could hardly believe that the Israelites had sent a boy without armor or shield to fight him. "Are you trying to mock me?" he cried out. "If you come any nearer you will be food for the dogs and jackals."

David rose to Goliath's challenge. He shouted, "You have defied the name of the Lord God of Israel. He will deliver you into my hands today, and it is your body that will be cut down, not mine. In life you have defied God, but by your death all the nations of the world will see God's power and greatness."

After he had finished speaking David slipped a stone into the slingshot, aimed, and sent the stone flying into the air. It hit Goliath right in the middle of his forehead.

Immediately Goliath fell to the ground. David then cut off the huge man's head. Everyone in the Israelite camp, as well as all of the Philistines, marveled at what God had accomplished through David, the young man who depended on God.

Meeting God

Remember the Promises
"Trust in the Lord with all your heart and lean not on your own understanding; in all your ways acknowledge him, and he will make your paths straight." *Proverbs 3:5-6*

Grow in God's Love
Was David braver than King Saul? How could David be so confident? What are some situations in which we need to depend on God?

Pray
What difficult things must you do in the next few days? Ask God to help you through those times of hard work, temptation, or stress.

God Protects His People

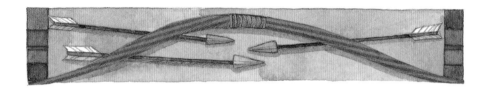

It is no secret that Christians have enemies. The world doesn't understand our close relationship with God and tries to come between us. Satan is prowling around like a hungry lion, seeking ways to snatch us from God's loving arms. Sometimes we even have to fight with ourselves — when we know what God expects of us, but sin seems more fun and exciting.

Without God's protecting arms around us, we would surely die.

David and Saul

1 Samuel 18-20

Saul couldn't believe that Goliath was dead — killed by someone who had been just an unknown shepherd a short time ago. It had looked so effortless. Maybe he should have dared to fight Goliath himself. But Saul didn't want to appear jealous of a mere boy. He made David the leader of 1,000 soldiers in his army and arranged for David to marry one of his own daughters.

The Lord smiled on David, and David always had success when he led his men into battle. David became an instant hero among all of Israel. One day Saul heard women in the streets singing about David's victories, saying, "Saul has killed his thousands, and David his tens of thousands." Saul was enraged that he was no longer the people's favorite. He hated David from that day.

Fortunately, David had a friend in the house of Saul. Jonathan, Saul's son, had loved David from the day he had watched him defeat Goliath. And God used Jonathan to protect David from Saul's anger. One morning Saul told all the leaders of his army, including Jonathan, to seek out David and kill him. Jonathan went out and warned David to stay away from Saul until it was safe. Then he returned and tried to talk reasonably to Saul, reminding him that David had always been loyal to him and had risked his life over and over again on the battlefield. Saul listened to his son and vowed that he would not kill David.

But not long afterwards when David was in Saul's chambers, Saul was once again overcome by fury. He threw a spear that he was holding right at David and nearly pinned him to the wall. Once again God protected David from Saul. David was able to avoid the spear and escape to his own home.

As long as David stayed near Saul, his life was in danger. One day he found his friend Jonathan and asked, "Why is your father so angry at me? What have I ever done to deserve this treatment?"

Jonathan did not want to say bad things about his own father and tried to defend Saul to David, but David could not be convinced. "Soon it will be time for Saul's festival of the New Moon," David said. "I will stay away. If your father asks where I am, tell him I've gone to Bethlehem to make a sacrifice. If Saul shows any anger, you will know that he still wishes to have me killed. If he is not angry, then I will be safe."

Jonathan agreed that this was a good test of Saul's mood. And he promised to tell David as soon as he could if Saul intended to harm him. He took David out into a nearby field and showed him a good hiding place. "I will shoot three arrows," he told David. "If the arrows fall between me and you, then it is safe for you to be with Saul. But if the arrows fly beyond the spot where you are hiding, then your life is in danger and you must flee."

On the first night of the festival, Saul was busy and didn't appear to notice David's absence. But on the second night he came up to Jonathan and asked, "Where is that young man from Jesse's family?"

Jonathan told him what David had suggested, that David had gone to Bethlehem instead of staying in Jerusalem for Saul's feast. Saul's reaction was what David had expected. "You have been protecting him!" he exploded at Jonathan. "Don't you see that he is threatening our kingdom? Don't you see how he has taken the love of the people away from me? Go and find him, for he must die!"

It was a strange feeling for Jonathan to disobey his father, but he remembered the promises he had made to David. He went to the field where he knew that David was waiting and shot three arrows far into the distance, way past the place where David was hiding.

Then David came out to him, and the two friends wept together. "You were right," Jonathan told him. "My father's anger against you is great. You can never come back to his court."

David and Jonathan promised again that they would always remain faithful to each other. Then David, knowing that God would continue to watch over him, left Jerusalem in secret.

Meeting God

Remember the Promises
"You are my hiding place; you will protect me from trouble and surround me with songs of deliverance." *Psalm 32:7*

Grow in God's Love
What are some of the ways God protects us? What people take care of you? What are some ways God can use you to care for other people?

Pray
Thank God for protecting you and being a hiding place for you.

God's People Worship

Stained glass windows. Banners. An organ. A choir. Bells. Guitars. Incense. Candles. Chanting. Hand clapping. Silence. Which of these are part of your worship in church?

Christians worship God in many different ways. In fact, if you were to go to a church very different from your own, it might be hard for you to stop thinking of the differences between that church and yours and to see instead the Lord who is at the center of worship in both churches. When we approach God, Jesus said, the important thing is not style or tradition. The important thing is having a pure heart.

David

2 Samuel 6-7

Saul died on the battlefield while surrounded by the army of the Philistines. He was a very unhappy and troubled man. He knew that he had displeased the Lord again and again. He knew that his throne would be taken from his family and given to David, whom he hated.

Upon Saul's death, David was anointed king. He was the people's favorite — a brave military leader, a convincing speaker, and someone who was not afraid to be open about his trust in God.

As soon as King David had made his borders safe and gained the loyalty of all twelve tribes of Jacob's family, he worked to bring the ark of the covenant to the capital city, Jerusalem. The ark was the special box that the Israelites had made to hold the stone tablets God had given to Moses. The glory and power of God rested upon the ark. David wanted it to stay in Jerusalem and to become the focus of worship for the entire country.

After some problems along the way, the day finally arrived when David led the procession of the ark through the city gates. David was so overcome with emotion that he took off his royal robes and sang and danced and clapped his hands and leaped for joy. He was celebrating God's faithfulness to the nation and also to himself.

His wife, Michal, the daughter of Saul, did not share David's joy. All she could think about as she watched the celebration from her window was how improper it all was. Certainly her father had known his place as king. Saul would never have let all the young people of the city see him behave like that.

When David returned she accused him of being an unfit king. But David would not listen to her. "It was not your father or any other man who made me king. It was the Lord alone, and he is the one who is to be praised. Even though I am king of Israel, I am the Lord's servant. He is my king, and I will worship him."

Later on, as David looked around him in his beautiful cedar palace, he was struck that while he had a permanent place to live, the ark of the Lord was only in a tent. He called the prophet Nathan to him and said, "I will build a temple to the Lord fitting for his glory."

That night the Lord spoke to Nathan and told him what to say to David. "I have never asked the sons of Israel to build me a house of cedar. I am the one who has established David on his throne. And I am the one who will build his house — a great family. David's son, not David himself, will build a temple for me."

When David heard these words the next day he was overcome by feelings of thankfulness and praise before the God who had blessed and guided him. He said:

Who am I, Lord, that you have brought me this far, to be king over your people, and
  to be the father of kings?
There is no one like you, O Lord God, for you have chosen a small nation, taken
  her out of captivity and blessed her with health and safety.
You are great and awesome.
You are the sovereign, Almighty God.
There is no one like you.

Meeting God

Remember the Promises

"Sing joyfully to the Lord, you righteous; it is fitting for the upright to praise him. Praise the Lord with the harp; make music to him on the ten-stringed lyre. Sing to him a new song; play skillfully, and shout for joy." *Psalm 33:1-3*

Grow in God's Love

What is your favorite part of your church's worship? What is your favorite song of praise? Are there parts of a worship service that you think should never be changed? Ask an older person what worship services were like when he or she was young.

Pray

David thanked and praised God for God's promises to make his kingdom great. What are some things for which you can thank and praise God? Be specific in your prayer today.

God Corrects His People

We don't like to think about God's anger. It is pleasant and reassuring to remember that God loves each one of his people and always wants the best for us. And of course those things are true. But it is also true that God gets angry when people keep turning away from him. Noah witnessed the force of this anger as his evil generation was overwhelmed by the flood. Abraham saw God's fury unleashed against the wicked cities of Sodom and Gomorrah. And sometimes God must punish the people he loves to remind them to turn their hearts back to him.

David

2 Samuel 11-12:14

David was the best king that the nation of Israel ever had. He was a great military leader and also a wonderful example of a person who put God first in his life. He had a close relationship with God, and his people saw that he spent much time in prayer. They learned the poems and songs he wrote that praised God.

Because he was the king, David had almost everything that he wanted. His servants prepared delicious banquets for him to eat. He wore the finest robes of anyone in the country. He had jewels, horses, chariots, and close friends. All the people of Israel loved and respected him. Here was the kind of king they had hoped for years ago when Samuel anointed Saul as king.

David loved God deeply, but his heart was not completely focused on God. When temptation came to him, David did not resist it. One day as he was walking in his gardens, David saw a beautiful woman in the courtyard of the house next to his. She was, in fact, the most beautiful woman David had ever seen. And David wanted to marry her. But that was impossible, since she already had a husband.

David knew and respected Bathsheba's husband, Uriah. He was a good man and an important general in Israel's army. Now, however, David saw Uriah as an obstacle that was preventing him from marrying Bathsheba. David went back inside and thought about how he could get Bathsheba to be his wife. If only Uriah were dead, David thought, Bathsheba would be free to marry him. Yet murder is a sin — David couldn't possibly kill Uriah. Then David thought about how dangerous Uriah's job was. Perhaps one day Uriah would die on the battlefield.

Soon David's thoughts grew darker. No one would know if David sent Uriah to a very dangerous part of the country. Uriah might not die there, David thought, but if he did David could take his beautiful neighbor as his own wife. He sent for his messenger and gave the order for Uriah to be assigned to a place where his life was at great risk.

It wasn't long before David's selfish desires were realized. Bathsheba became a widow and was free to marry him.

No one in Israel could ever prove that David had arranged to have Bathsheba's husband killed. In fact, no one suspected it. War was a dangerous thing, and men who fought were often badly hurt or killed.

But God knows the secrets hidden in everyone's heart. He knew that David had been selfish in his love for Bathsheba. He knew that in order to get what he wanted David had become a murderer.

God sent the prophet Nathan to the court of King David to confront him. Nathan told David a story.

"There is a very poor family in your kingdom who have little to make them happy. With each new day the rising sun finds the couple already awake and working, and they are working still when the sun goes down. Even the children of that family must help carry water, prepare meals, and help farm their small plot of land. There was only one thing in life that made the family happy — a lamb. They cared for it and treated it like a pet.

"Now there is also a rich man who lives near that family. He has many flocks but does not care for any of them as deeply as the poor family cares for their lamb. One day the rich man had a guest come for dinner. A very important guest. Naturally, the rich man wanted to make a good impression on him. So he said to his servant, 'Fetch me a lamb for dinner. But don't take one of mine. Take the one from that poor family that lives about a mile away. They owe me a debt, anyway.' So the lamb was taken from the poor family and eaten at the rich man's table."

When Nathan finished the story, King David's face was red with anger. "Tell me, Nathan, who this selfish, rich man is. He deserves to die!"

Nathan pointed a finger at King David. "You are the man. You took Bathsheba when you had other wives, just as the man took that lamb when he had so many others. You must humbly ask God's forgiveness for this sin, for God's anger with you is great."

Meeting God

Remember the Promises
"My son, do not despise the Lord's discipline and do not resent his rebuke, because the Lord disciplines those he loves, as a father the son he delights in." *Proverbs 3:11-12*

Grow in God's Love
Why do parents punish their children? How do you feel when someone talks to you about your mistakes, the way Nathan talked to David?

Pray
Have you ever felt like David, who, even though he had so much, wanted even more? Ask God to help you appreciate all the many gifts he has given you.

God's People Confess

We know how God wants us to live. He gave us directions for living a life that pleases him, and he sent Jesus to show us an example of a perfect life. Yet no one obeys God completely. No one has a life that is free from sin.

What do we do when we have disobeyed God? Do you ever try to cover up your mistakes so no one else will find out about them? Do you ever pretend that they didn't happen? Or, do you ever hide from God by not talking to him and not listening to his word? What does God want us to do when we have done something wrong?

David

Psalm 51

When Nathan was finished talking, David was speechless. His sin had been found out. God saw not only the things that he had done. God also saw the motives and attitudes in his heart.

David knew that he could no longer hide from God, and he didn't want to. He wanted to be happy in God's presence the way he had always felt before. He didn't want any barriers to come between himself and the Lord. Nothing — not even the beautiful Bathsheba — was more important than that relationship.

David found a quiet place where he could be alone and talked to God. He said:

I need a new heart, Lord, because mine is full of sin.
Make me clean inside and keep my spirit right with you.
I have done a terrible thing and it has hurt and disappointed you.

I have done things that you know are wicked.

Please don't send me away from your presence.

Don't take away the strength and comfort of your Holy Spirit.

I want to be joyful in your company, the way I was when I first came to know you.

Please watch over me, so I never again wander away from you.

Meeting God

Remember the Promises

"If we confess our sins, he is faithful and just and will forgive us our sins and purify us from all unrighteousness." *1 John 1:9*

Grow in God's Love

Since God already knows what we have done wrong, and has forgiven us because of Jesus' death, do we need to tell him about our sins? What happens when we try to hide our sins from God?

Pray

As you pray today, remember that God wants you to be honest when you talk with him.

God Provides
for His People

Rain. Sunshine. Fertile soil. Fuel. Shelter. Clothing.

All these things — or the things we need to make them — are sent by God. Every time we turn on a water faucet or pick up an apple, we can remember that God is the one who takes care of us.

In our daily lives when things are going well for us, we often forget that God is the one who provides for us. We feel as if we can take care of ourselves. But when we go through hard times, God sometimes gives to us in ways we think of as miracles. When we see such wonders, we cannot ignore the fact that they come from God and that he is the one who is fulfilling our needs.

Elijah and the Widow of Zarephath

1 Kings 17

The prophet Elijah lived in Israel during a time of great wickedness. The king, Ahab, set a bad example for everyone else by worshiping wooden or metal idols. He didn't have room in his life for the one true God. Because God was so displeased with Israel's disobedience, he let a terrible famine fall on the land. There was little anyone could do to keep from going hungry during those years.

Elijah was hungry just like everyone else in the country and wondered how he would find enough to eat. Then God showed him a special place by the river Cherith where he stayed for many weeks. What a delight it was for Elijah to be in that cool, quiet place at a time when the rest of the land was dry and parched! In the morning ravens brought Elijah a meal of bread and meat, and in the evening they brought another meal.

Elijah drank water from the river, so all his needs were cared for. The time Elijah spent by the river was a special time for him to talk with God and trust God for each morsel of food and sip of refreshing water.

When the river dried up after a time, God told Elijah to go to a town named Zarephath, where he would meet a widow. This woman would feed Elijah, God said, until the rain returned to water the land. Obediently, Elijah walked through the dusty countryside to Zarephath. Everywhere he looked he saw skeletons of sheep and parched crops. The drought had caused tremendous destruction during the time Elijah had been beside the river.

When Elijah came to Zarephath he met a woman gathering sticks for firewood. Elijah asked her for some water and bread.

"I have no bread," she told him. "Only a little flour and a few drops of oil. I was just collecting some wood to make a fire to bake my last loaf of bread from that small amount."

"Go home and make a small loaf for me," Elijah told her, "and afterwards you can make some more for yourself and your son. And the God of Israel will keep your oil jar and your bowl of flour full as long as this drought continues."

The woman went to her home, wondering about Elijah's instructions. She wasn't sure that she believed in his God. Could he truly give her the food that Elijah had promised? Wouldn't she be crazy to share what little she had with this stranger who came begging for food?

But the widow did as Elijah had told her. She kneaded together the flour and oil and a little water, then baked it over the fire. She took the loaf to Elijah, who was still waiting at the place they had met. Elijah received the bread thankfully, knowing that God had again kept his promises to him.

When the woman returned home she checked her storage containers. She expected them to be empty — no one in Zarephath had anything extra. Even if they had wanted to, no one could have come to restock her kitchen while she was gone. But somehow, Elijah's words had come true! The jar was heavy when she lifted it, full to the brim with thick oil. And in the bowl was a generous heap of flour. The widow gasped in amazement, touched the flour and oil, and tasted them. She thought of the beggar, Elijah, who had spoken to her. "Truly he was a man of God," she said. And she knew, without a doubt, that God had worked a miracle in her kitchen.

Meeting God

Remember the Promises
"And my God will meet all your needs according to his glorious riches in Christ Jesus."
Philippians 4:19

Grow in God's Love
What does the word "prophet" mean? Why did God send prophets to Israel when he did? What messages did they bring?

Pray
Think of people in other parts of the world or in your own church or neighborhood who are hungry. Ask God to provide for their needs today.

God's People Rejoice

When you sing "Joy to the World" at Christmastime, what do you think about? Maybe in December the joys that we think about most are family gatherings for meals or presents or quiet candlelight church services. But we have many other experiences on earth that cause us to rejoice. Think of playing outdoors on the first day of summer vacation. Or hearing your teacher say "Good for you!" when you do well on a test. Or running home on a deep fly to left field while your coach cheers.

All of these joys are real and wonderful. But they cannot compare with the joys we will experience when "heaven and nature sing" in God's kingdom.

Isaiah

Isaiah 55

Israel was in trouble. The kingdom was divided into two parts. The northern part, ruled by kings who followed false idols, did not worship the one true God. They had forgotten the one who had created them, brought them out of slavery, and provided for all their needs.

The southern part of Israel was usually more faithful to God. They trusted him for their victories in battle. They believed that he was their provider and that he alone was worthy of their worship. But a time came when even these faithful Israelites were thinking of idols. They were wandering away from their belief in God alone.

God sent a prophet named Isaiah to the Israelites. He spoke God's words to all the people, pleading with them to turn to the Lord. "If your hearts are not pure and totally focused on God," he told them, "the country itself will collapse. You will have no power against military forces that threaten to cross your borders. Soon the Babylonians will carry you away, and you will live just as you lived in Egypt — strangers in a land that does not honor God."

Isaiah was heartbroken when he saw his friends and neighbors in Israel turn their back on his words, for they were really turning their backs on God. He saw all the wonderful gifts that God was offering His people. But he also saw how Israel was looking instead for something cheap and glittery that would not last. Isaiah pleaded:

> *If you are thirsty, come to the waters God provides for you.*
>
> *If you are poor, come to the table God is setting and eat freely.*
>
> *God is offering you food and drink at no cost.*
>
> *Look at you!*
>
> *You spend money on things that can never satisfy your real hunger.*
>
> *You are working for wispy possessions that you cannot hold onto;*
> > *see how they disappear with the wind?*
>
> *The Lord is near — seek him.*
>
> *If you are doing evil, turn from your sin and look to the Lord.*
>
> *He will forgive you and shower you with mercy.*
>
> *Look at how the rains wash and refresh the earth.*
>
> *God's word is just like that: he speaks and all the earth responds in love and praise.*
>
> *One day all the earth will burst with joy, and everyone will know the peace of God.*
>
> *Even the hills and mountains will resound with singing,*
> > *and the trees everywhere will clap out a steady rhythm of praise.*

Meeting God

Remember the Promises

"This is the day the Lord has made; let us rejoice and be glad in it." *Psalm 118:24*

Grow in God's Love

What do people today look to for satisfaction? Are these good things or bad things? How can we possess the joy and completeness that Isaiah described?

Pray

"Lift up your heart, lift up your voice, rejoice, again I say rejoice" is the chorus of an old and well-loved hymn that calls Christians to praise. Pray a prayer that expresses the joy of knowing Christ.

God Loves His People

The people of Israel believed that they knew God. They had memorized God's laws. They knew many stories about how God had helped them and led them through difficult times.

But the law and the stories were not enough. The people of Israel did not live the way God wanted them to live. They stole from other people. They did not share their possessions with others. They loved themselves more than God. God saw that they were blind — as blind as people from other nations who had never heard of the one true God.

So God sent a light to help all his people to see.

Jesus

Luke 1:26-56, 2:1-7

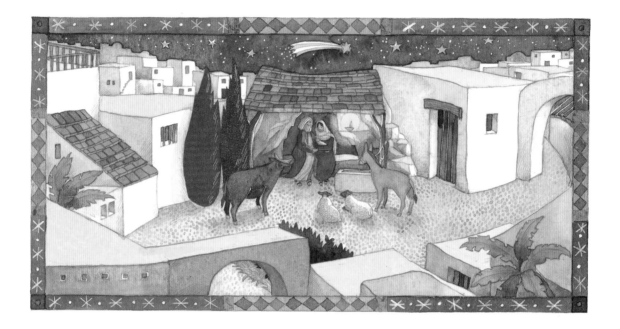

A young woman named Mary lived with her parents in Nazareth. She planned to be married to Joseph, a good man who cared for her. He earned his living by building things. Mary knew that her life soon would be filled with cooking, cleaning, carrying water, and taking care of her husband. It was the life lived by all the women of Nazareth.

Yet God had more plans for Mary, plans that would set her apart from all her friends and from all women in all times and places. One day God sent a special messenger, the angel Gabriel, to tell her of his marvelous plan.

"You have lived in a way that pleases God," Gabriel told Mary. "He is going to send his Spirit upon you, and you will conceive a child. That child will be God's special son who will save people from their sins."

At first Mary was speechless with surprise and wonder. She could not understand this strange announcement. Yet she dared to believe what she could not understand. Humbly she told Gabriel, "I am a servant of God. He may do with me as he wishes."

When Mary told Joseph about Gabriel's visit, he was even more surprised than she had been, and he found it hard to understand God's plan. They were not married yet — how could Mary be expecting a child?

God comforted Joseph by appearing to him in a dream. "Do not abandon Mary," God urged Joseph. "She will need you to help raise the child. The baby she is carrying is my Son, but I have chosen you to be his earthly father." Then God told Joseph to name the baby Jesus, which means "Savior."

When the time for Mary to have her baby was drawing closer, Joseph learned that they would have to travel to Bethlehem. The Roman governor had passed a law that all citizens of Israel must sign up in the city of their ancestors to pay taxes.

So they made their way to Bethlehem. When they neared the city they joined a great number of other travelers — people who, like themselves, had come to pay their taxes. Inside the gates of the city Mary and Joseph found a great mass of people, clamoring and scrambling, searching for a place to stay for the night or trying to buy food and water. Joseph joined the crowd. He knocked on door after door up and down the streets of the city, asking — then begging — for a place to stay.

Finally, Joseph found someone who offered him shelter in his stable. "It is not much," the innkeeper apologized. "But it will be protection from the wind and rain." Even though it was not what they had hoped for, Mary and Joseph were relieved to have a roof to shelter them and the soft beds of hay to rest upon.

And that very night the miracle happened. It was what the angel Gabriel had announced, what had frightened Joseph, and what Mary had looked forward to with awe and gladness. The Son of God, Jesus, the Savior, was born in the rough stable of Bethlehem.

It wasn't a grand entrance into the world. Jesus came the way all other babies come, because he was human, just like other babies. In a year or two he would learn to walk and talk. He would fall and get bruised and scraped up when he chased around with the neighbor children in Nazareth. He would be hungry and thirsty and grow tired after a long day of work in Joseph's carpentry shop.

Yet this small baby who lay at Mary's side was also God's message to the world. He was the light God sent to help us to see. He was the word that told us about God's love. What a glorious, incredible gift!

Meeting God

Remember the Promises

"For God so loved the world that he gave his one and only Son, that whoever believes in him shall not perish but have eternal life." *John 3:16*

Grow in God's Love

Around the world Christians celebrate Christmas in many different ways. How do your family and your church celebrate Christmas?

Pray

Thank God for sending Jesus to be the light of the world. Ask him to shine in the dark places of your life and in the dark places of the world.

God's People Seek Him

Have you ever spent a long time working on a puzzle and when you put in the last piece you had you found that there was still an empty space remaining? Remember how incomplete the picture looked? Remember how frustrated you felt that you couldn't find the last piece you needed in order to finish it? Perhaps you spent the rest of the day looking for that missing puzzle piece.

When people look for God, they should be even more eager than someone who looks for a toy or a lost coin or even an expensive jewel. Finding God is the most important thing we will ever do.

The Shepherds and Wise Men

Luke 2:8-20, Matthew 2:1-13

On the night that Jesus was born, a group of shepherds were sleeping under a clear and starry sky near Bethlehem. Suddenly the stars in the sky grew dim, and a glorious angel appeared. The shepherds all woke up in astonishment. They turned toward the angel, then shielded their eyes from its brilliance.

"Don't be afraid of me," the angel told them, "for I have good news for you and for all people. A king has been born this very night — a king who will be your Savior and Lord. Go and search for the baby and worship him. You will know him when you find a baby wrapped in cloths and lying in a manger."

When the angel was finished speaking, he was joined by a huge number of other heavenly messengers. They all joined in singing their praise: "Glory to God in the highest, and on earth, peace." The song was clear and pure; more beautiful and holy than anything the shepherds had ever heard. "Glory to God," the song rang out.

When the angels returned to heaven and the stars once again looked bright in the night sky, the shepherds followed the angel's directions and looked for this newborn holy child. The shepherds were unaccustomed to the city of Bethlehem, but at this time of night the streets were quiet. The citizens and travelers were deeply asleep in their homes or makeshift shelters. Even though the shepherds were usually shy, they took courage from the hymns of the angels to awaken strangers and ask them for directions to a stable where a new baby rested.

And so it happened that they came to the stable where Mary and Joseph gazed in wonder at their new son. The shepherds knelt around the manger. One of them reached a thick, bramble-scarred finger to touch the soft infant hand. Another clucked his tongue softly, as if calling to one of his own newborn lambs.

In a land far distant from Bethlehem some Magi, people who studied the stars, noticed a new star, one they had never seen or heard about. "What could this mean?" they wondered. Being men of wealth, they could afford to leave their homes and travel a great distance to find out the truth about this strange new star. They organized their caravan as quickly as they could, gathering servants, food, charts, and gifts, then headed west in the direction of the star.

After many weeks their journey led them to the court of King Herod in the city of Jerusalem. "We have seen a new star," one of the Magi told Herod. "We believe it is a sign that a new king has been born to the Jewish nation. Tell us where we can find this king, for we are on a quest and want to worship him."

These words shocked and disturbed Herod. He had no idea that a new king had been born. It certainly was no son of his. Would this king try to take away his power? Herod called together the learned men of the temple and asked them where it was believed that the promised Messiah would be born.

The Pharisees did not even have to open a scroll for they knew each letter of all the prophesies. "From Bethlehem," they told Herod, "will come the one who is to be shepherd to the people of Israel."

Herod turned to the Magi who had come miles across the eastern desert. "Start looking for the child in Bethlehem," he told them. "And when you have found him, tell me where he is." He looked at the Magi closely and gave a sly smile, then added, "so that I, too, may worship him."

When the Magi left Herod's court they followed the star to Bethlehem and kept their eyes on it until it rested over the place where the Jesus was. They got down off their camels and, with unfamiliar humility, knocked upon the door.

Joseph welcomed them, and they bowed down before the child. They gazed in wonder on this child that had caused a star to break forth from the heavens. Then the Magi opened their travel packs and presented the gifts they had brought for Jesus — gold, frankincense, and myrrh.

God warned the Magi not to return to Herod, who was not at all interested in worshiping Jesus but wanted to harm him. God also told Joseph that he needed to take Mary and Jesus to a place where they could be safe from Herod's jealousy and anger. So Jesus spent his first years in the country where his ancestors had experienced their many years of hardship and slavery — Egypt.

Meeting God

Remember the Promises
"You will seek me and find me when you seek me with all your heart." *Jeremiah 29:13*

Grow in God's Love
Where are some places you can search for God? What things or people can assist you in your search?

Pray
Ask God to give you a heart that longs to know him and for a strong spirit that will keep searching even when the journey seems long.

God Asks His People to Repent

When you apologize to a friend for something you did or said, it should mean that you wish you hadn't done or said it. When you tell your teacher that you're sorry you didn't do your homework, it should mean that you intend to work hard on your next homework assignment.

When we meet with God we need to be sorry for what we have done that has caused our relationship to be broken. We ask God to forgive us for the things we have done that make him sad. But we need to do more. God wants us to turn away from our sin and to try our hardest not to let sin back into our lives.

John the Baptist

Luke 3:1-18

Jesus had a cousin, the son of Zechariah and Elizabeth, whose name was John. John lived a simple life in the wilderness, eating a diet of only locusts and honey. He loved God, listened to his voice, and tried to live a life that was pleasing to him.

After many years, John came out of the wilderness to preach to the people of Israel. "Repent of your sins!" he challenged them. "Be baptized to show you mean to live a new kind of life. The Lord is near. Make your hearts ready for his coming! He is your long-awaited king who brings salvation!"

John looked around him and saw the crowd he had drawn to him, people who took great pride in their nation's history of faith. "Don't believe that you will be saved simply because you are children of Abraham," he warned them. "Listen well. God is able to change these lifeless stones into children of Abraham. Repent of your sin, and live a life that shows you have truly repented." John's voice became louder and firmer. "God is like a gardener, ready to prune away any tree that doesn't produce good fruit. Look at your lives. See what kind of fruit you are bearing."

"We don't understand," the crowd told him. "What is this fruit?"

"You must stop being greedy and learn to share, for a start," John said.

Some tax collectors gathered together and wondered, "Would you call us greedy? Sharing just isn't part of our job." One of them dared to ask John, "Hey, Prophet. What does repentance mean for us?"

"Don't take more than is fair," John answered, "and don't keep the extra for yourself."

Finally, some soldiers came to John and asked, "What about us? Can we also have this good fruit you're speaking of?"

John knew the temptations that soldiers faced. "Don't take advantage of your strength," he said. "Be content with your pay, and don't force those who are weaker than you to give up what you don't have a right to take."

News of John's preaching spread quickly in Israel. John was surrounded by crowds wherever he went. Each week more and more people sought him out and heard his challenging words.

"Who do you think he is?" the people asked each other. "Is he Elijah come back from heaven?"

"No," some said. "He is greater than Elijah. He must be the Messiah — the anointed one sent from God."

John heard the rumors about himself and responded, "I am not Christ. When he comes, he will baptize you with fire and spirit, not with water, the way I do. I am not worthy even to stoop down and untie his sandals. But I tell you the truth — he is near. Be ready! Watch!"

Meeting God

Remember the Promises
"Repent, then, and turn to God, so that your sins may be wiped out. . . ." *Acts 3:19a*

Grow in God's Love
Can you think of any prophets of our society, people who bring God's word to this generation? What kinds of fruit do you think we can expect when we turn away from sin? (See Galatians 5:22-23.)

Pray
Thank God for the new life that he has made possible for you.

God's People Turn to Him

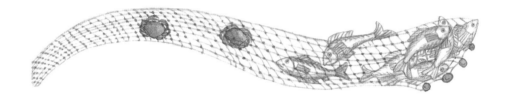

Sometimes when a new person comes into your life you change. A new teacher may get you excited about a subject that you were never very interested in before. With a new friend you may discover new ways to have fun. A new coach may help you become a better athlete.

In even more dramatic ways, when our lives are touched by God we become different people.

The Disciples

John 1:40-42

Andrew was a good fisherman. Ever since he was a curious child old enough to leave his mother, he had watched the daily harvest of fish from the Sea of Galilee. He knew the deep places of the sea where the fish liked to gather. He knew about boats and nets and hooks. He was familiar with the tug of his muscles when the nets were full and also the feeling of defeat when the catch was a poor one. And Andrew knew how to read the skies. He could predict coming storms and knew when it was safe to be out on the lake and when he must find safety at shore.

Andrew was also a religious man. He prayed each day and looked expectantly for the Messiah — the one God had promised would fill David's throne.

One day as Andrew was working on the shore he was thinking about this Messiah. Could it be that John the Baptizer was the chosen one? Only yesterday Andrew had heard him speak his message of repentance. He spoke with the power of

God. Even though he didn't look like Andrew's idea of a king, perhaps he was truly the Messiah.

Then Andrew saw the shadow of someone coming towards him. When he looked up to see who it was, he saw a man smiling at him. "I see that you are a fisherman," the man said to Andrew. "Follow me, and I will show you how to fish for people."

"To fish for people?" Andrew repeated. "I don't understand."

But Jesus told him simply, "Come."

Here was a man of power, Andrew knew. Someone like John, but gentler, more holy. He couldn't describe it any more clearly than that. And neither could he ignore him. Andrew's eyes never left Jesus as he sprang up to follow him down the shoreline. He didn't think about the equipment he left behind or the life he was also leaving.

But later that afternoon he returned to the place where Jesus had found him, the place that had been his family's spot for generations. His brother, Peter, was there now, sorting his catch and preparing to take it to market.

"Peter!" Andrew exclaimed. "I met an incredible person today. He said he can teach us how to fish for people."

"What can he mean by that?" Peter asked his brother. "How can you catch people?"

"I'm not sure," Andrew answered. "But I know that after being with him for only part of a day, my life will never be the same. He seems to know everything about me. Come with me and judge for yourself. I am convinced that Jesus from Nazareth is the Messiah!"

Peter looked at the piles of fish he had made on the shore, at the nets that needed to be inspected and folded, at the boat that he and Andrew had patched only last week. Then, leaving it all behind, he walked with Andrew to find this man, Jesus.

Meeting God

Remember the Promises

"Therefore, if anyone is in Christ, he is a new creation; the old has gone, the new has come!" *2 Corinthians 5:17*

Grow in God's Love

Can you think of any examples of people whose lives were changed when they came to know God? Do changes happen instantly for a new Christian, or do they take time? Should we expect someone who meets Jesus to change occupations or careers like Andrew and Peter did? What are some other changes that a new Christian experiences?

Pray

Ask God to show you if there are attitudes or habits in your life that you need to change as you continue your walk with Jesus.

God Heals His People

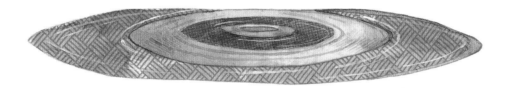

Do you remember what it feels like to have a bad cold? Maybe your throat or ears ache. You feel miserable. And thinking about your cold makes it difficult to think about other things, like your schoolwork, your friends, or even God.

Many people in Israel were ill, suffering with problems much worse than a ten-day cold. Jesus saw people who couldn't hear or see, people who had never walked, and people who had an awful disease called leprosy. He wanted to make them whole, free from pain, so they would know him and praise him and glorify him.

The Man beside the Waters

John 5:1-15

When Jesus began his ministry, sick people started coming to him to ask him for healing. Often large crowds of people who needed his help crowded around him. And Jesus healed those who came to him, sometimes working through mealtimes or late into the night.

Once when Jesus was in Jerusalem near the temple he and his disciples were by themselves. The crowds had left them for a while. Jesus came to a pool that some people believed contained special healing water. When the water moved in a certain way, according to the belief, the first person to enter the water would be healed of his or her illness.

Jesus looked at the people gathered by this special pool and noticed in particular a man who was unable to walk. Jesus knew that it had been many years since injury or disease had caused this man to be paralyzed, and Jesus felt very sorry for him. He wanted to make the man well. Yet he didn't just stretch out his arms to heal him. First he asked the man if he wanted to be healed.

"Yes!" the man exclaimed from his bed by the water. "I have been lying here for years, hoping that I might be healed of my crippling illness. But someone else always gets to the pool first. Each time the waters move, it's as if a race is starting. I have no one to carry me down into the water when it begins to churn, and I cannot get there on my own strength."

The paralyzed man had answered Jesus' question well. Jesus knew that he was eager to be free of his disability. In a strong voice he told the man who had not walked in thirty-eight years, "Get up. Pick up your mat. Leave this place behind you."

Could it be that easy? Was it possible that he could walk without first swimming in the miraculous pool? Slowly the man sat up. Then, feeling new strength in his legs and arms, he pulled himself up off the ground. He was standing! What joy he must have felt to be relieved of his suffering after so many years!

The man picked up his bed and walked away from the place where he had lain for so long. As he walked he thought about the healer who had noticed him. And he remembered his own words, "I cannot get there on my own strength."

Meeting God

Remember the Promises
"Praise the Lord, O my soul, and forget not all his benefits — who forgives all your sins and heals all your diseases, who redeems your life from the pit and crowns you with love and compassion." *Psalm 103:2-3*

Grow in God's Love
How does God heal people today?

Pray
Pray for people you know who have an illness or are recovering from an injury.

God's People Ask

  Angels don't need to ask God for anything. They spend all their time praising God and being messengers of his glory.

  But we are not angels. We are people who need money for next week's groceries or for last month's heating bill. We need courage to face things that frighten us, comfort when someone we love dies, and love for people who tease us or ignore us.

  Because people have so many needs, we need to pray.

The Lord's Prayer

Matthew 6

When Jesus began his ministry he knew that the people of Israel had badly damaged their relationship with God. They still believed in him, but they didn't talk with him as if he were their special friend and helper. Instead, they were using their prayer time to show off to others. They would stand up in the middle of town and pray in loud voices using long, fancy words. Whoever heard these prayers would think, "That person must be very holy because he recites such beautifully-worded prayers."

But Jesus had a different way of measuring a person's goodness. He taught his disciples that God doesn't look at outward appearances. God is not impressed by anyone's language or voice. God wants to see a sincere, pure heart.

Jesus told his followers to find a quiet place to pray so that they could be alone with God. He told them to pray simply and honestly and to remember that the purpose of their prayers was to be heard by God, not to be seen by other people. God knows what our needs are before we say them. We make ourselves look silly when we try to hide them, or when we try to pretend before our all-knowing God that we are superhumans who can take care of ourselves.

"Look at the lilies growing in the field," Jesus told his disciples. "God gives them robes of splendid beauty. They don't work for wages or do anything to earn this blessing, but God is delighted to give it to them. Your heavenly father is even more happy to give you, his children, the things you need."

Jesus looked into the faces of his disciples and saw that they still did not understand his message. "See the small sparrow over there?" he asked them. "God knows when it flies up against the wind and when it falls again to the earth. If he takes care of such a small part of creation, he will also care for you. He is willing to give you so much, if you only ask him."

The disciples were still confused. So Jesus gave them an example of a simple and honest prayer that they could use as a model for their own prayers.

Father in heaven, you are holy.
Please rule in our hearts and in the world,
so that we always act in ways that make you happy.
Please provide for our daily needs,
and show us mercy as we try to show mercy to others.
Keep us from doing and thinking evil things, and protect us from harm.
You are a powerful and glorious king, now and always.
Amen.

Meeting God

Remember the Promises

"Ask and it will be given to you; seek and you will find; knock and the door will be opened to you." *Matthew 7:7*

Grow in God's Love

What are some of the things we ask God for? Is praying the same thing as giving someone a list of things you want for your birthday?

Pray

Jesus said, "God is like a father. What earthly father do you know that would give his children stones when they asked for bread?" When you talk with God today, remember that God is your loving heavenly father who never gives his children stones.

God Teaches His People

When Jesus began to work as a healer and preacher many people called him "Rabbi." But Jesus was a different sort of teacher than anyone in Israel had seen before. He didn't stay sitting in the temple or synagogue. He didn't just talk about God's law. He was an example of someone who obeyed the law each minute of the day. He was a model of a perfect, sinless life. Those who heard him speak or saw how he cared for the people who crowded around him never forgot the lessons that Jesus taught.

A Parable

Luke 15:11-32

Jesus told this story that describes how God will forgive us if we are truly sorry for our sins.

A rich man had two sons who helped him take care of his land and livestock. The brothers knew that one day, when their father died, they would divide his property between them and they would be very wealthy.

One brother grew tired of waiting. He didn't exactly wish that his father were dead, but he didn't want to continue any longer his years of hard work on the family's land. He went to his father one day and said, "I know that half of all you own will one day belong to me. Please let me have the money now, so I may go and begin a new life for myself somewhere else."

The father loved his son and wanted to please him, even if that meant saying goodbye to him. He had his stewards count out the great sum of money that he had planned for his son to have at his death. He gave the gold and silver pieces to his son and with great sadness watched him pack his belongings.

While the father and his other son turned back to their responsibilities, the foolish son traveled a great distance to faraway cities. He spent his father's money on sumptuous feasts and expensive pleasures. He bought himself fine clothes and gave away fancy gifts to impress the new friends he made.

It wasn't long before the son noticed that his supply of money was running out. But instead of planning how he could save some of it, he simply continued having a good time no matter what it cost.

The end of the money came sooner than the rich man's son could imagine. Now he had to support himself by working. But the only job he could find in that far-off country was taking care of the pigs of a mean-spirited farmer. Even though he worked harder than he ever had before, the son made hardly any money. The only food he had on some days was the corn meant for the pigs.

Finally he began to realize how greedy he had been. He recognized that his father had been very generous with him and had always shown love to him. He knew that his father was a good man who treated his lowest servant kindly. Surely if he returned to him as a servant, the son thought, he would at least receive a set of clean clothes and good food to eat. With a mixture of fear and hope the son set out in the direction of his home.

The father had not forgotten his beloved son, and he hadn't stopped loving him. Every day the son was gone the father looked down the road, wondering what had happened to his son and if they would ever see each other again. The father was overjoyed when he saw his son returning to him. Quickly he ran to meet him and welcomed him home with great joy. He ordered his servants to slaughter a lamb for a great feast to celebrate his son's return.

The other brother was amazed at these events. "I've been here helping you faithfully all the years my brother was gone," he told his father, "yet you never gave a feast in my honor! Why is this brother of mine treated so lavishly, as if he had never wasted your money or dishonored you?"

It was hard for the father to explain himself to his faithful son. "Maybe you will understand when you yourself are a father," he said. "I thought that your brother was dead, but today I have discovered that he is alive! Your brother realizes that he was wrong, and he has asked for my forgiveness. What kind of a man would I be if I could not forgive my own son?"

Meeting God

Remember the Promises

"I will instruct you and teach you in the way you should go; I will counsel you and watch over you." *Psalm 32:8*

Grow in God's Love

How do you learn something most easily? By reading about it? Listening to someone explain it to you? By watching someone else, or trying it yourself? Think of a teacher who helps you learn. What makes that teacher a good teacher?

Pray

Ask God to give you a willing mind to learn the things God wants to teach you this week.

God's People Believe

All these stories tell us that God is a God that can be trusted. He supplies food to the hungry. He heals those who are sick. He protects his people from their enemies. He saves his people from their sins. David wrote many poems that express his trust in God. "The Lord will achieve for me the things that I need," he wrote in one poem. In another he said, "He has given angels the job of watching over me. They guard me and sustain me and keep me from harm."

Each of us has our own story to tell about how God has worked in our lives. God calls us, his children, to him one by one. But each of us must learn the same lesson as everyone else — God is the only one who can help us in times of trouble; God is the only one who can give us eternal life.

Nicodemus

John 3:1-21

One of the important Jewish leaders in Jerusalem was Nicodemus. He had heard many rumors about Jesus. People were saying that he could make lame people healthy. He could cure fevers and make blind people see. Nicodemus heard people talk about the wonderful things Jesus was teaching — that God looked at a person's heart, not just at his or her behavior, and that God wanted his people to call him "Father."

Nicodemus wanted to meet Jesus for himself and see if the rumors about him were true. He wondered if Jesus could possibly be the promised Messiah. The other Jewish teachers would be angry if they knew he were visiting Jesus, so Nicodemus went to him at night when no one would see him.

"Teacher," he began, "I know that you have been sent from God. No one could do the miraculous things you have done without God's help."

Jesus didn't directly respond to Nicodemus's words. Instead, he told him what was important for him to hear. "Unless people are born again, they cannot see the kingdom of God," he said.

"What!" exclaimed Nicodemus. "How can someone be born a second time? Can I go back to my mother's womb to emerge again?"

"No," Jesus replied patiently. "There is the physical birth that everyone experiences. And there is another birth, a birth of the spirit. If you do not experience that second birth, you will not see God's kingdom."

"I don't understand!" Nicodemus thought of the scriptures he knew so well. Nowhere did they mention being born again. "How do you achieve this second birth?" he asked.

Jesus answered, "It is a gift of God, given through the Holy Spirit. And it is given to everyone who believes that God sent me to save them from their sins."

After their meeting Jesus and his disciples continued their ministry among the people of Judea. But what happened to Nicodemus? Did he become a follower of Jesus? Did he recognize him as the Messiah? Did he ever experience the second birth Jesus offered to him?

The Bible gives us strong hints that he did. When the Pharisees were talking about Jesus among themselves and beginning to plan for his arrest, Nicodemus was willing to support Jesus in public. He urged the other Pharisees to listen to what Jesus taught before they judged him. And when Jesus died, Nicodemus brought expensive spices to prepare his body to be buried.

Meeting God

Remember the Promises
"Trust in the Lord with all your heart and lean not on your own understanding; in all your ways acknowledge him, and he will make your paths straight." *Proverbs 3:5-6*

Grow in God's Love

Is belief in God an easy thing or a difficult thing for you? What are some other things or people that we put our trust in?

Pray

The thing that most often stops us from trusting God is fear. Tell God about the things you are afraid of, and ask for God's help as you learn to trust him.

God Knows His People

If someone wanted to write a biography of you, he or she might talk first to your friends to find out what you like to do, what subjects you enjoy, and what kinds of books you like to read. The writer might talk to your neighbors to hear stories about you and your family.

But if the writer really wanted to know the kind of person you are, he or she would want to interview your mother or father. One of your parents could tell the writer what you were like as a baby and toddler, whether you were content or fussy, adventuresome or shy. Your mom or dad could describe the situations that make you tense and what makes you really happy — all the characteristics that make you the wonderful individual that you are.

Yet not even your mom or dad knows you as well as God does.

Peter

Matthew 26:17-35

The stress had increased with each day. The Jewish leaders were stirring up anger against Jesus. Peter didn't understand why Jesus had brought them to Jerusalem. Why couldn't they have stayed in the hills of Galilee where they were safe and welcomed?

To be honest, nothing could compare with the welcome Jesus had received just a few days ago when he had come into the city. He was riding on the back of a donkey he had somehow found. And that in itself was strange, for all their traveling over the past three years had been done on foot. When he entered the gates, the crowd that was gathering to celebrate the holy days was overwhelmed with excitement. They recognized Jesus as the Messiah. "Blessed is he who comes in the name of the Lord!" some shouted. "Hosanna, hosanna, hosanna!" The children waved palm branches and scattered them on the path in front of the donkey.

But the welcome hadn't lasted. And tonight their time together in that upstairs room had been so strange. Peter didn't understand what was happening, but every detail seemed to carry enormous meaning. After they finished the traditional Passover meal, Jesus took a piece of the unleavened bread and broke it. He said that it was his body, broken for them. Then he took a goblet of wine and sipped some. It was deathly quiet now. No one whispered a word. Then Jesus passed the goblet to the disciples and said in a sad, strained voice, "This is my blood, shed for you."

"What does it all mean?" Peter wondered to himself. They were walking now along the dark path to Gethsemane. Jesus had told them he needed a quiet place to pray.

Peter tried to remember all the things Jesus had told them about what was to happen. "If I am lifted up from the earth I will draw everyone to myself." And, "If you destroy the temple I will raise it up in three days."

But these teachings were crowded from his mind by the image of Judas at tonight's supper. "One of you will betray me," Jesus had told his group of friends. "Surely not, Lord!" they had all said, almost in unison. And Jesus was quiet, looking at them all with his piercing gaze. "Is it I, Lord?" John had asked. "Is it I?" the others echoed.

Jesus said simply, "It is the one to whom I give this bread." And it was Judas. Judas, Peter's friend. The practical one who had been like an anchor to this small group. The one who always seemed to know the directions to the next home or town they were traveling to. The one who took care of their tiny budget. But now Judas's face was twisted and dark. Peter had never seen him — had never seen anyone — look like that. "Do what you have to do," Jesus had told him. And Judas sprang up from the table and ran out.

Later, as they all were leaving the room, Peter had gone to Jesus' side and said, "I could never betray you, Lord." He expected Jesus to put his arm around him and say something like, "I know I can always count on you, Peter." But instead Jesus had said, "Ah, Peter, you sound so bold. But I tell you truthfully that before the cock crows in the morning you will have denied me three times."

Deny him three times? It was impossible! What did all this mean?

Meeting God

Remember the Promises

"O Lord, you have searched me and you know me. You know when I sit and when I rise; you perceive my thoughts from afar." *Psalm 139:1-2*

Grow in God's Love

How does it feel to know that you cannot hide from God, to know that God knows all there is to know about you? Do you feel fearful? Or, do you feel dearly loved?

Can you imagine any time when you might be tempted to deny that you are a friend of Christ?

Pray

Thank God for knowing you and calling you by name.

God's People Remember Him

Some things are easy to remember. Your birthday, for instance, or how to ride a bike or jump rope. Other things aren't so easy. You forget when your library books are due, or you forget how to spell a hard word.

God understands that people forget things. He is patient and loving when we make mistakes, but God wants to help us remember the important things of our faith. God knows that if we forget about Jesus' death we will begin to lose our love for him. God knows that if we forget about his resurrection we will begin to lose our hope.

Peter

Matthew 26:47-58, 69-75

The worst possible thing happened. That same night after Jesus had been praying for awhile in the garden, the quietness of the garden was disturbed by the sound of many footsteps coming near. The quivering light of a lantern shone against the rocks. Then Judas came, leading several people sent by the temple high priests and even some soldiers from Rome. Judas went up to Jesus and kissed him.

"Seize him!" one of the leaders ordered the soldiers. "This is the Galilean who says he is the Son of God."

Peter wanted to fight them with all his strength. He tore a sword from the hands of a young Roman and slashed at the soldier's head, cutting off an ear. If Jesus weren't going to call down legions of angels to protect himself, then at least Peter would do his part.

"No, Peter," Jesus said firmly. "Not yet." And he reached out and put the ear back in place on the head of the Roman soldier. The ear was healed, just as though it had never been cut off. Then roughly, eagerly, the crowd seized Jesus and led him away from the garden to the court of the High Priest, Caiaphas. The disciples were dismayed and frightened. They ran away, leaving Jesus to face his accusers by himself.

But Peter followed the crowd to the temple. No one took any notice of him, for everyone's eyes were on Jesus. When Jesus was appearing before Caiaphas and the other priests and teachers and elders, Peter stayed outside in the courtyard with the soldiers, warming himself at a fire someone had built. Peter couldn't see Jesus or hear what he was saying. He heard only the murmur of the crowd and sometimes an angry shout.

A servant girl came to the courtyard and saw Peter. "Aren't you one of the followers of the man they are accusing?" she asked him.

"No," Peter told her. "I don't know who you're talking about. I'm just trying to stay warm." But he went away from the fire to avoid her searching look.

She found him only a few minutes later and said to the other people waiting in the courtyard, "This man was with Jesus."

"No. You're mistaking me for someone else!" Peter insisted.

"But you are from Galilee, like Jesus. Surely you know him," the girl pressed him.

And Peter lost control. "I don't know the man you're talking about!" he shouted. "Leave me alone!"

And immediately after Peter said that, a rooster crowed. Peter remembered what Jesus had told him at supper the night before, and he knew that Jesus had been right. Peter left the temple, weeping bitterly.

Meeting God

Remember the Promises

"I will remember the deeds of the Lord; yes, I will remember your miracles of long ago. I will meditate on all your works and consider all your mighty deeds." *Psalm 77:11-12*

Grow in God's Love

Two special ways that Christians have to remember the works and promises of God are the Lord's supper (communion) and baptism. How does your church celebrate these two events?

Pray

Thank God for sending Jesus to die in your place. Thank God for the ways he has taught you and guided you and for the people who have told you about Jesus.

God Saves His People

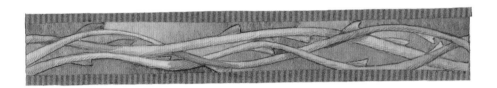

Even though God always loves his people and wants to forgive them, they still must be punished for their sin. Israel experienced great suffering under evil kings who did not honor God. Jonah spent three unpleasant days inside a great fish. From the time of Adam and Eve, people have known that any sin results in death.

Because God is completely good and holy, he could not overlook the sin of his children or pretend it wasn't there. But he thought of a way to carry the punishment for those sins and save his people from suffering and death.

Jesus

John 18:28-40, 19:17-42, 20:1-18, Matthew 28:1-15

Caiaphas and the religious leaders did not have the legal power to put Jesus to death. After they had questioned him they took him to their governor, Pilate. Pilate did not want to have anything to do with the matter, but he finally agreed to order Jesus' death to make the people happy. He took a basin of water and washed his hands in front of the people, as if to say, "See. I am washing myself of all responsibility for this man's death!" But the angry crowd only shouted, "Crucify him!"

In that place and time, criminals were punished by crucifixion. They were nailed to large wooden crosses and left to die. Jesus was not a criminal. He had never done anything wrong. But because of his great love for the world he let himself be nailed to a cross as if he were an evil person.

It was terrible for Jesus' friends and followers to watch Jesus die. They heard the Roman soldiers make fun of Jesus and throw dice to see who would take his robe. They watched as one of the soldiers gave Jesus some wine vinegar to drink. They heard Jesus tell John to look after his mother, Mary, as if he were her own son. And at the end of the long ordeal, they heard him cry, "It is finished."

When Jesus died it was late in the afternoon, almost the time for the Sabbath to begin. If Jesus' followers didn't bury Jesus' body quickly, it would have to remain on the cross until Sunday morning, the day after the Sabbath. The disciples quickly arranged for Jesus to be buried in a tomb owned by a wealthy friend of Jesus, Joseph of Arimathea. They watched as soldiers rolled a great stone in front of the tomb. Then the disciples all went back to their lodgings. The long and horrible day — the worst day in the history of the world — was over.

When the important Jewish leaders heard that Jesus was dead they thought that they had achieved what they wanted. Jesus would no longer be around to teach and heal and listen to people. When Pilate heard that Jesus was dead, he thought that he had succeeded in making everyone in Jerusalem happy, and that he, Pilate, would be more popular from now on. And when Satan saw that Jesus was dead, he thought that he had won a great victory in his ancient battle with God. The Son of God had been crucified.

But the story was not over.

On Sunday morning, the first day after the Sabbath, Mary Magdalene and a friend went to the tomb where Jesus' body had been buried. They took with them some ointments and spices to anoint the body. When the women neared the tomb they saw that the huge stone that had blocked the entrance to the cave had been rolled away. Sitting at the entrance was a glorious being that they knew was an angel.

"Are you looking for Jesus of Nazareth?" the angel asked them.

Too shocked to say anything, the women could only nod their heads.

"He is not here," the angel told them, and gestured towards the place the women had seen his body laid two days before. "He has risen from the dead. You must find his disciples and tell them what you have seen and what I have told you. And tell them to return to Galilee, where Jesus will meet them."

Mary watched the angel until it disappeared from sight, then turned away. "How could these things be true?" she wondered. She was certain that Jesus had been dead, yet the angel had said he was alive and was going to Galilee. What did it all mean?

Then suddenly she saw another person in that quiet cemetery. At first Mary thought he was only the gardener who tended the bushes and flowers, but there was something familiar about him. He reminded her of someone. And then the man called her name, "Mary." His voice was unmistakable. It was Jesus! The angel had not lied. Jesus was alive!

"Teacher!" she said joyfully. It was what she had always called him. She tried to hug him, but Jesus avoided her touch. "Don't cling to me now," he told her, "but go to find the disciples, and tell them that I have risen from the dead."

Mary ran to the city to tell Peter, John, and the others that Jesus was alive. The news spread rapidly to everyone whose lives had been changed by Jesus. Soon the story of Jesus' resurrection was being told everywhere — among the Pharisees, at the court of Pilate, and in every corner of Jerusalem.

Meeting God

Remember the Promises
"And everyone who calls on the name of the Lord will be saved." *Acts 2:21*

Grow in God's Love
What would the world be like if Jesus had not died and been raised from the dead? What would your life be like if you did not know Jesus?

Pray
Thank God for the changes he has made in your life. Thank God for sending Jesus.

God's People Come to Him

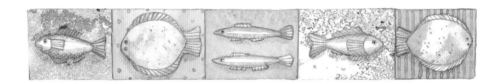

An eight-year-old boy hates to go out to the playground for recess because the other kids tease him. One day he wears glasses for the first time. The teasing gets worse and turns into punching and hitting. When the boy is about to fall to the ground, he sees his older brother come onto the playground — his brother who is on the wrestling team. What joy! Somehow the younger boy finds the strength to call his brother's name and run towards him.

When we recognize our Savior, we come to him with relief and gladness.

Peter

John 21:1-14

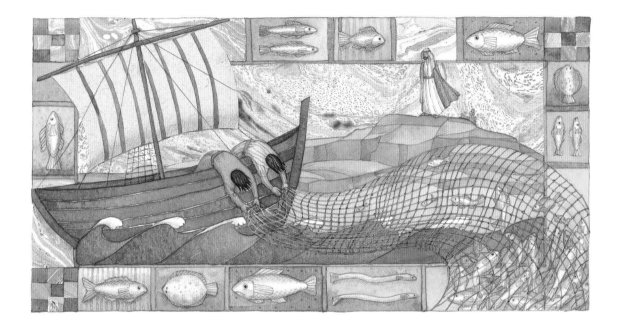

Waiting did not come easily to Peter. He hated sitting around doing nothing. He wanted to be out at sea, rowing against the wind, pulling his catch into his boat, or at least walking along the familiar paths of Galilee. He had stayed in Jerusalem for three days after Jesus' crucifixion, not knowing what to do with himself or where to go.

Now that he had seen Jesus alive, he still wasn't sure what he should be doing. He knew that this was an enormous thing he had seen — his teacher and friend returning from the grave. Yet Peter didn't know what was going to happen next. Was Jesus going to take up his old routines of teaching and healing? Was he now going to reveal himself as king of Israel? Peter was restless and impatient for answers.

Finally he persuaded some of the other disciples to go fishing with him. "We have to eat," he told them simply. They set out in their old familiar boat, but they didn't catch anything. They tried a different spot, but still the nets came up empty. Then one of them heard a voice calling to them from shore. "That man is saying something about putting our nets out on the other side of the boat," said one disciple.

"I don't see what difference that would make," grumbled Peter. But they all pulled in the nets from one side and dropped them in again on the opposite side.

Almost instantly a swarm of huge fish filled the net. "Where did these all come from?" the disciples asked each other. "A minute ago there was scarcely a minnow in sight, and now we have more than we could expect from a full day's work!"

They steered their suddenly heavy craft towards shore and the man who had given them such strange advice.

"Look!" John suddenly exclaimed. "It's the Lord!"

Peter didn't know how he could not have recognized him earlier. It was indeed Jesus. "Master!" he shouted joyfully. And "Hurry!" he prodded the others. But even before the word was out of his mouth he had gathered his robes about his knees and jumped out of the boat, running and kicking and splashing through the gentle waves, towards his Lord.

Meeting God

Remember the Promises
"Come to me, all you who are weary and burdened, and I will give you rest."
Matthew 11:28

Grow in God's Love
Read John 21 to find out what Jesus had to say to Peter after he came to him. What are some ways you can demonstrate your love for God?

Pray
One of the best-known hymns of faith is "Just As I Am." If you know the song, use it to begin your prayer today.

God Stays with His People

Have you ever wrapped a tiny present in a great big box? When the person who received it opened it, was he or she surprised to find something very different from what was expected?

The Bible, too, is full of unexpected events and facts. If you want to find your life you must lose it. Life comes from death. A baby born to poor travelers is really a king. And on the day when Jesus left his disciples, he promised to be with them always.

Jesus' Ascension

Matthew 28:11-20, Mark 16:15-20, Luke 24:49-51

The disciples had many questions to ask Jesus, but ever since his death and resurrection it was hard to find time with him. He came upon them without announcing himself, then left just as suddenly. He kept saying, "Don't you remember what I taught you?" But the problem wasn't in the remembering, it was in the understanding.

Jesus had appeared to them several times since that wonderful Sabbath morning. Peter and John and one or two others were beginning to realize that his resurrection meant that their lives would never be the same. Even Thomas, who had doubted earlier, recognized that his friend and teacher was also his Lord and his God.

One day Jesus told the eleven disciples to go to Galilee and to wait for him on top of one of the highest hills there. They had been there with Jesus before. As they walked together they recalled happy memories of their three years with Jesus. They also spoke of the rumors that some of the temple authorities were spreading. They were saying that Jesus had not risen from the dead, but that his disciples had stolen his body from the garden tomb and buried him someplace else. And the elders and priests bribed the Roman soldiers with money so they would tell the same story to anyone who asked.

When Jesus met his followers on the top of the mountain he said to them, "Go, and tell the stories and teachings to everyone you meet. Baptize those who believe in the name of the Father, the Son, and the Holy Spirit. Never forget my commandments."

Then Jesus looked at his friends that he loved so dearly. "Even though I am leaving you, I am always and forever with you," he told them.

And when he had finished speaking, Jesus was taken up into heaven, leaving only the echo of his words, "always and forever."

Meeting God

Remember the Promises
"And surely I am with you always, to the very end of the age." *Matthew 28:20b*

Grow in God's Love
What are some of the ways God is with us today? How does he teach us, help us, and guide us?

Pray
When Jesus ascended into heaven he knew that his disciples didn't understand everything about him. But he knew that they had enough knowledge to begin to teach others and to spread his love. Ask God to help you know how to serve him, too.

God's People Meet Together

Even though we come to God one by one, it is very unusual for Christians to remain alone. God knows that we need each other for help and comfort. He likes to hear us worshiping and praying together and to see how we love one another.

Some churches have auditoriums that seat 2,000 people or more; others are small converted stores or businesses. And in countries where the government is opposed to religion, Christians have to meet quietly and privately. The place or style of worship does not matter. What is important is that people who love God have a way to encourage each other and worship together.

The Early Church

Acts 1:10-26

The disciples watched Jesus going up to heaven and kept looking at the sky long after a cloud had blocked him from their view. Suddenly two heavenly beings came to the disciples. "Why are you people of Galilee looking up into the skies? Jesus will come back in the same way that he left, but not for a long time. Remember his words to you. Go back to Jerusalem, and wait there until God's power comes upon you."

So the disciples returned to Jerusalem, the city where they had experienced such great sorrow and also unspeakable joy. They waited together in an upper-level room they found, similar to the one where they had shared the Last Supper with Jesus. The disciples that Jesus had called to follow him were joined by some of the other men and women who knew him, including Jesus' mother Mary. Some of the time they spent recalling the stories Jesus had told them and the wonderful things that he had done. But most of the time they prayed. Often one of the disciples would lead them all; sometimes the room was completely quiet as they prayed silently.

Then Peter stood up and said, "We number only eleven disciples now, since Judas is gone. With the money the priests gave him for betraying Jesus, Judas bought a field where he killed himself. We should replace him with a person who has been with us since Jesus was baptized and began his ministry. Who do you think we should call?"

The others proposed two names, Joseph and Matthias. The disciples prayed that God would show them which of the two he had chosen to take the place of Judas. Then they cast lots, the way Jewish people had done for centuries when they asked God to reveal his will.

The lot fell on Matthias, who became one of the twelve, an apostle and also a leader of the church of Christ.

Meeting God

Remember the Promises

"For where two or three come together in my name, there am I with them." *Matthew 18:20*

Grow in God's Love

What do you like best about your church? The worship services? The friends you see there? The people who teach you and the stories you hear? The projects people work on together? To have a strong church, is any one of these things more important than the others?

Pray

Ask God to show you how you can serve your church family. Thank him for the special friends that you have at church.

God Gives Power to His People

Even though God is all powerful, he doesn't want us to be afraid of him. He doesn't want to be unapproachable. God wants to be a part of our lives every day. He sent Jesus to take away the sin that separated us from him. And God sent the Holy Spirit to live in our hearts, so that we can talk to God at any time and feel his presence and love and power.

The Holy Spirit

Acts 2

On the special Jewish holiday of Pentecost the twelve apostles were still gathered with other believers in a large room in Jerusalem. It had been several weeks since the events of the Passover weekend. The believers were trying to be patient. They weren't even sure what they were waiting for. "The Holy Spirit will come upon you," the angels had told them on the mountain when Jesus left. The words were unfamiliar to them, yet they carried with them great hope.

Suddenly the apostles heard a loud noise like the sound of a powerful windstorm. Then tongues of flames came down on each believer. Immediately each of them was able to speak in a foreign language. It was a strange yet joyous experience. The room that had been quiet for so long was now filled with a jubilant mixture of languages. Everyone there was smiling, laughing, crying, and praising.

Outside, the streets were crowded with Jewish people from faraway countries who had come to Jerusalem to celebrate the festival of Pentecost. Soon, a large knot of people gathered outside the building where the disciples were meeting. The visitors to Jerusalem were curious about the voices coming from the inside. Some of them recognized the language of their own country and listened carefully as the story of Jesus' life, death, and resurrection was proclaimed.

When the followers of Jesus came outside and continued to speak in these foreign languages, the people were confused. "How is this possible?" they asked. "How did you country people learn to speak so many different languages? Or are you all drunk with holiday wine?"

Peter stood up and told the crowd, "It's only nine o'clock in the morning! We are not drunk. We have been given power from the Holy Spirit. That power enables us to speak in other languages. It is the same power that raised Jesus from the dead."

Then the message of God's salvation — the story of all that Jesus had done and all that he had been — spilled from the lips of the believers. Three thousand people came to believe in Jesus that day, and they all confessed their sins and were baptized.

The day of Pentecost was only the beginning of the apostles' ministry. Because of the power of the Holy Spirit, the good news spread to all parts of the Mediterranean world, into Africa, into Asia, and the ends of the earth.

Meeting God

Remember the Promises
"The Lord, the Lord, is my strength and my song; he has become my salvation."
Isaiah 12:2b

Grow in God's Love
One of the most famous hymns of the church says, "God in three persons, blessed trinity." What are the three persons of God? Can you think of an example of anything that has three parts but is still a unity or whole?

Pray

God sent his Spirit to the early Christians to strengthen them for the task of telling other people about Jesus. The Spirit gives us power for other tasks as well. Think of something you have to do this week, and ask God for the Holy Spirit's help.

God's People Tell Others about Him

Some people talk all the time. You know the kind of person. She sits down on the bus beside you and tells you that she made an Indian bracelet yesterday and plans to go to the Grand Canyon next summer and is having a hot dog for lunch today. For people like this, talking about God might be easy. If their church is having a special program for kids, they might enjoy going around the neighborhood inviting everyone to come.

Other people are more quiet. It is sometimes hard for them to find the words they need to express an idea. They may worry about how other people will react to what they say. It might take them two days to build up their courage to invite their best friend to that same church program.

No matter which kind of person you are, if you believe in God you want others to hear about him and to know his love.

Saul

Acts 9:1-31, 16:16-40

Saul was a Jewish leader who lived in the time of Jesus. After Jesus died, Saul was eager to make people forget about him. He went from town to town where he heard that followers of Jesus were gathering in churches. He had those followers thrown into prison. One day as he was traveling to Damascus, a powerful light surrounded him, and he fell to the ground in fear. A voice so loud that even Saul's companions could hear it asked, "Saul, Saul, why are you persecuting me?"

"Who are you, Lord?" Saul asked in reply.

"I am Jesus of Nazareth whose followers you are putting in chains," the voice answered. "I have a plan for your life. Go into Damascus, and I will tell you what to do."

When Saul got up from the ground he could not see anything. It was as if he had been blinded by seeing and hearing Jesus. His traveling companions had to guide him into Damascus by holding onto his arm.

For three days he waited to hear what God wanted to tell him. He was too unsettled to eat or to drink. Meeting Jesus made him realize that everything he had done over the last several months to stamp out the growing church was wrong.

A Christian named Ananias lived in Damascus. One day when he was praying he had a vision of Jesus. The Lord told Ananias that Saul was in Damascus and that he was to go to him and tell him that God had a special purpose for his life.

Ananias was astounded. "Is this the same Saul that has been going from church to church, arresting believers and putting them in prison?" he asked.

"Yes," Jesus answered. "But he is the one I have chosen to take my word far across the world. He will be a great ambassador for me, teaching people everywhere about my love."

Ananias listened and obeyed. He found Saul, still blinded, and talked to him a long time, telling him about Jesus. Saul, with a believing heart, listened to the story of Jesus' death and resurrection. He heard Ananias tell him about God's plan for his life. Before he left, Ananias touched Saul's eyes, and once again Saul was able to see.

Saul, who was now called Paul, wanted the whole world to know about Jesus and that Jesus had died to save people from their sins. He wanted to tell people how God had spoken to him on the road and that his life was now very different than it had been. Paul went to the synagogues of Damascus, telling the Jews who gathered there that the God they worshiped had revealed himself in Jesus. Then he traveled to distant places telling everyone he met — not just Jewish people — about God's love.

One day Paul and his partner, Silas, were preaching in Philippi. A slave girl who was very troubled came near to them. She earned money for the people who owned her by telling fortunes. Paul knew that a demon controlled her. God gave Paul the power to send the demon away, and the slave girl was healed.

But when the demon left her, the girl was no longer to able to tell fortunes. Without that ability her owners would be unable to earn money. Enraged, they took the Christians to court. The judge ordered Paul and the others to be beaten and sent to jail.

When God saw that the group of Christians were in prison he caused a large earthquake to shake the jail. The doors of the building were thrown open. The chains that held the prisoners against the walls were loosened. Nothing was now keeping Paul in prison.

The guard who was in charge of the group of prisoners saw the open door and was terribly afraid. He was responsible for keeping the prisoners in jail. If he failed to do that he would be punished harshly. Instead of facing the anger of the town, the guard decided to kill himself.

Yet when he neared the jail cell he heard voices. The prisoners were still there! They had not escaped. Instead they were praying and singing in thanksgiving to God. Paul called out to the guard, "Don't harm yourself! Silas and I are still here. You have done no wrong."

The jailer was astonished that the two men hadn't run away, and he was moved by their joy and faith. "Sirs," he asked them, "what do I have to do to be saved?"

Paul responded with the simple words, "Believe in the Lord Jesus Christ."

The jailer at Philippi heard Paul's words with an open heart, and he believed them. He accepted the wonderful love of Jesus for him.

Paul and Silas stayed in prison for a few more days, and their new friend did not lose his job. And when they were released from prison, Paul and Silas didn't stop inviting all who would listen to believe in Jesus.

Meeting God

Remember the Promises
"Therefore go and make disciples of all nations, baptizing them in the name of the Father and of the Son and of the Holy Spirit, and teaching them to obey everything I have commanded you." *Matthew 28:19-20a*

Grow in God's Love
What are some ways that your church spreads the message of God's love to other people? What are some ways that children and young people can help?

Pray

Does your church support any missionaries? Pray that God will help the missionaries as they tell people about his love.

God Encourages His People

Behind every good athlete is a great coach. When you watch an Olympic ice skater leap and spin and dance, think of the person who has been at the practice arena with the skater for hours and years of hard practicing. When you watch a track record being broken by a new star, think of the coach who keeps telling the athlete, "You can do it; try one more time."

Christians sometimes feel discouraged. The job of spreading God's good news in a dark world isn't an easy one. Yet God doesn't expect us to work alone. He encourages us by the comfort of the Holy Spirit. He gives us friends who share our burden. And every time we read his word, he speaks to us, telling us not to give up and to keep our hearts focused on him.

Paul

Philippians 1

When Paul traveled around the Roman world, he led a great number of people to Christ. Many were glad to hear the news of God's salvation and to accept God's love. Paul and the other apostles began new churches in places like Corinth, Ephesus, Thessalonica, Philippi, and Rome.

But Paul's preaching also got him into trouble over and over again. The Roman authorities were angry that Paul didn't let his followers worship gods like Zeus, Venus, and Mars any longer. Christians, Paul said, must worship the true God alone. The Jewish leaders were angry that Paul was preaching that God had sent Jesus to be the Messiah.

Paul got into trouble wherever he went, but he didn't let that keep him from preaching. Whenever he was ordered to appear before a council of priests or a Roman magistrate to answer questions about his faith, he answered everything they asked with great boldness. "My life has been changed because of Jesus," he said. "Jesus has shown us the way to God; now we can come to God without fear. We can call him 'Father.'"

Often the scene before the officials ended with the official ordering Paul to be put in chains and led off to prison. But even during his weeks of imprisonment, Paul found a way to keep doing his work of ministry. He preached to his jailors, as he did at Philippi when God miraculously loosened his chains and unlocked the prison doors. And he wrote letters to the dear friends he had left behind in other cities.

Paul didn't always have an easy message to send the new churches. "Stop fighting!" he told the Corinthians. "You all believe in Christ. Be grateful for what you can do for him. Don't try to puff yourselves up all the time." "You aren't remembering what I taught you," he told the Galatians, "but are following other teachers. Stay with what you know to be the truth."

But Paul's letters were mostly filled with wise words that the churches needed to hear. "God's grace is tremendous!" he told the Romans. "It covers all our sin. If you believe in your heart that Jesus is Lord and can tell others of your faith, you will be saved. Nothing can ever separate us from the incredible love of God."

"I am so proud of you," Paul wrote to the Philippians. "I am happy every time I think of you, and I pray for you every day. Keep on putting your trust in God, and he will surround you with his peace."

God has used the letters of Paul to encourage generation after generation of Christians. When we read his words, we can hear God encouraging us today.

Meeting God

Remember the Promises
"Do not be anxious about anything, but in everything, by prayer and petition, with thanksgiving present your requests to God. And the peace of God, which transcends all understanding, will guard your hearts and your minds in Christ Jesus."
Philippians 4:6-7

Grow in God's Love

What are some of the times when you need words of help or encouragement? What are some ways that you can encourage other people?

Pray

Thank God for the gift of his word, the Bible, that both teaches and encourages us.

God's People Give

God has given us many wonderful things — our homes, our schools and churches, our friends and families. One of the ways we can thank God for these blessings is to give him something in return. The ancient people of Israel chose an animal to be sacrificed to God on an altar. In Jesus' day, a poor widow gave the very last coin she had to the priests at the temple. Giving has always been an important way that we worship God.

Another way that we honor God is by sharing with other people. When we know that our lives belong to God, we understand that everything we have also belongs to him. Instead of hoarding our money and possessions, we use them to help other people. This is how we show the world that Jesus loves them.

Dorcas

Acts 9:36-43

In the town of Joppa lived a woman named Dorcas who loved God very much. When she heard about Jesus, she believed in him and trusted that he would save her.

Dorcas also loved other people. She liked to help them with their chores, and she prepared meals for them when they were sick. She was a good seamstress and often made clothes for new babies in the neighborhood or for others who needed them. Everyone in Joppa knew that they would always be welcome at the home of Dorcas. She would listen to them if they had a problem or cheer them up if they were sad.

One day Dorcas became ill. In those days doctors didn't have the strong medicines that we have today. No one knew how to make Dorcas well. Before her friends had time to understand what was happening or even to say good bye, Dorcas died.

A great crowd met in Dorcas's house. All the people whom she had helped were gathered there, sharing stories of what she had done.

Someone sent for Peter, who now was the leader of the Christian community. When Peter arrived, the grieving friends were gathered around the bed of Dorcas.

"This was a special woman!" they told Peter.

One of her friends held up some small dresses and tunics. "These are the clothes she had just finished making for some poor neighbors," she said.

"She nursed my mother-in-law every night when she was ill," one woman said, "so that we could sleep."

Peter was moved by the love these people had for Dorcas. He knew that she had earned that love with all her many acts of kindness. He asked everybody to leave the room. Peter knelt by Dorcas's bed and asked God to raise her up. Then Peter said, simply, "Get up, Dorcas."

And Dorcas opened her eyes.

She looked at Peter and realized what had happened. She had been dead but was now alive again!

With a broad smile Peter went to the door and called the friends of Dorcas. "Come and see what God has done!" he told them. "The woman you love is alive!"

Meeting God

Remember the Promises

"All the believers were one in heart and mind. No one claimed that any of his possessions was his own, but they shared everything they had." *Acts 4:32*

Grow in God's Love

Dorcas was known in all her town as someone who gave to others. What do you think you are known for? What would you like to be remembered for?

Pray

Paul wrote that the Lord loves a cheerful giver. Ask God to give you a glad heart as you learn to share what you have with other people.

God Gives Promises to His People

When Noah left the ark to walk in a world that seemed to be remade in beauty, God promised him that he would make sure that the sun would always rise and set and that harvest would always follow planting season. When Abraham walked away from his homeland to an unknown future, God told him that he would make a great nation from his offspring. He promised Moses that he would lead Israel out of the desert. God promised David that Israel's throne would always belong to his family. He promised Mary that her son would be the Savior of the world. Jesus promised his disciples that his death would not be the final word, but that it would draw people everywhere to fellowship with God.

And he promised to come back.

Jesus

John 14:1-7, Matthew 24:29-31

Well before he was arrested, Jesus had known that the time for his death was coming closer. Jesus had known that the days that lay ahead would be difficult for his disciples, that their grief would cause them to make wrong decisions, and their faith in him would grow weak. So Jesus had reassured them with precious promises.

"Don't worry," Jesus had told his followers. "Put your trust in me. I am going to be with my father. I will get your place ready too, so that when it is time we can be together. I'll come back for you. You know the way."

Thomas hadn't understood. Once again it seemed as if Jesus was speaking in riddles. "We don't even know where you're heading, Jesus! How can you expect us to know how to get there?"

Patiently, Jesus had explained it one more time. "I myself am the way, and the truth, and the life. I am the way to the Father. Think of all the things I have told you."

Jesus had continued to reassure the loyal ones who had been with him throughout the wonderful years of his ministry. "I know there are hard times ahead when I am away. But great things will come out of the suffering, and one day I will come back to you." Then Jesus had described a scene that the disciples could barely picture in their minds, but that they yearned for with all their souls.

"The expanse of the heavens will be darkened. The lights of the sun, moon, and stars will go out. And then the Son of Man will appear, and out of the darkness he will come in great glory and power, and all the nations of the earth will see him and bow down to him."

"Now come," Jesus had beckoned to them. "We must go to the garden."

Meeting God

Remember the Promises
"Holy, holy, holy is the Lord God Almighty, who was, and is, and is to come." *Revelation 4:8b*

Grow in God's Love
Why do you think God hasn't told us the exact time, or even the approximate time, that Jesus will come back? What things are more important for a Christian than guessing about dates?

Pray
John's final words in Revelation are "Amen. Come, Lord Jesus." Use those words in your prayer today.

God's People Live with Hope

There are many things about the future that are unknown to us. You don't know yet if you will be a doctor, a teacher, or something quite different. You don't know if you will get married, or to whom. But it is hope that helps us stay courageous and faithful as we carry God's promises with us into the days that lie ahead of us. With the eyes of faith there are important things about the future that we can know for certain.

Jesus

Acts 1:1-11

When Jesus went up into heaven a short time after the resurrection, his disciples were terribly sad. In spite of all the promises Jesus had given them they didn't know how they could get along without their beloved friend and teacher. It seemed as if their lives were over.

Then an angel came to them and said, "Why are you just standing around staring into the sky? Jesus has truly gone, and you can't see him anymore. But one day he will come back to earth in the same way that he left."

The followers of Jesus began to remember what Jesus had told them. "He promised that the Son of Man would come down from the sky with great power and glory," one of them recalled.

"And he said that no one would know the time that he would come," remembered another.

As they returned to the city from the mountain where Jesus had left them and as they continued their journeys to distant lands, the disciples were strengthened by those promises.

Our hope is that Jesus will come to earth again and rule as king. We know this will happen because God has promised it. We are not just dreaming or wishing to see him.

Our hope is that everyone will gather before Jesus' throne and acknowledge that he is Lord. Our hope is that God will wipe all our tear-stained faces and that we will never again experience sorrow or sadness.

Our hope is that one day we will walk with God as closely as Adam walked with him in Eden.

And it's a sure thing

Meeting God

Remember the Promises
"Now faith is being sure of what we hope for and certain of what we do not see."
Hebrews 11:1

Grow in God's Love
Have you ever thought you felt hopeless when you were really sad or scared? What are some ways that we can build up Christian hope in ourselves and in other people?

Pray
Thank God for promising us that he will come again and we will live with him forever.